How to Plan CHILDREN'S LITURGIES

By Mary Kathryn Machado

Published by
Resource Publications, Inc.
160 E. Virginia St. #290
San Jose, CA 95112

Editorial Director: Kenneth Guentert
Production Editor: Scott Alkire
Book Design: Christine Benjamin
Cover Design: Joanne Hawkins
Appendix Art: Audrey Marilyn Munoz
Mechanical Layout: Geoff Rogers and Agnes Hou

ISBN 0-89390-074-5
Library of Congress Catalog Card Number 86-060892
Printed and bound in the United States 5 4 3

Copyright © 1986 by Resource Publications, Inc. All rights reserved. For reprint permission, write Reprint Department, Resource Publications, Inc., 160 E. Virginia St. #290, San Jose, CA 95112.

Contents

1. Introduction 1
2. How to Plan Children's Liturgies 5
    I. Why Do We Pray?
    II. Overview of the Mass
    III. How to Use This Book
    IV. Lesson Planning
    V. Parts of the Mass
    VI. Theme
    VII. Theme Development
    VIII. Invitations
    IX. Mass Booklet
    X. General Guidelines for Typing the Mass Booklet
    XI. Timeline
    XII. Decorations
    XIII. Songs
    XIV. People Responses
    XV. Penitential Rite
    XVI. Prayers
    XVII. Readings
    XVIII. Response
    XIX. Homily
    XX. Creed
    XXI. Prayers of the Faithful
    XXII. Offertory
    XXIII. Eucharistic Prayer
    XXIV. Sign of Peace
    XXV. Communion
    XXVI. Blessing
    XXVII. Dismissal
    XXVIII. Closing Remarks
3. Conclusion 39
4. Review of Related Literature 41
5. Bibliography 45
6. Appendix 49
7. Additional Ideas 76
8. Planning an Entire School Celebration 90

*This book is dedicated to
John and Eileen Machado*

*Thank you Mom and Dad
for all your love and support
always*

Introduction

The Mass or Eucharistic celebration is the focal point of the Catholic faith. It is the most important prayer used in the Catholic Church. "Nothing is more evidently at the core of the Christian life than our public worship — which, in fact, is precisely what liturgy means" (Abbott, 1966, p. 134).

The National Catechetical Directory for Catholics of the United States, *Sharing the Light of Faith* (1979), clearly defines the Eucharistic celebration:

"The Eucharist is a memorial of the Lord's passion, death, and resurrection. This holy sacrifice is both a commemoration of a past event and celebration of it here and now. Through, with, and in the Church, Christ's sacrifice on the cross and the victory of His resurrection become present in every celebration. The Eucharistic celebration is a holy meal which recalls the Last Supper, reminds us of our unity with one another in Christ, and anticipates the banquet of God's kingdom. In the Eucharist, Christ the Lord nourishes Christians, not only with His word but especially with His body and blood, effecting a transformation which impels them toward greater love of God and neighbor...

"The Eucharist is also a Sacrament of Reconciliation completing and fulfilling the Sacraments of Initiation. In each Eucharist we reaffirm our conversion from sin, a conversion already real but not yet complete. The Eucharist proclaims and effects our reconciliation with the Father. 'Look with favor on your Church's offering, and see the Victim whose death has reconciled us to yourself' " (p. 69-70).

When the Catholic Bishops wrote the National Catechetical Directory, they recognized the special needs of young people. "Children often cannot participate fully in adult liturgies because they do not understand the words and symbols used or understand them only imperfectly" (p.77). And so the Bishops promulgated the *Directory for Masses with Children* in 1973. This directory encourages educators to combine liturgy and prayer experiences with the children's educational programs.

Young people who express their belief in God by writing their own prayers and choosing their own songs for Mass celebrations are living their faith. The *Directory for Masses with Children* (1973) states: "A fully Christian life cannot be conceived without participation in the liturgical services in which the faithful, gathered into a single assembly, celebrate the paschal mystery. Therefore, the religious initiation of children must be in harmony with this purpose" (paragraph 8). The children show by word, action and song what they believe. The Mass becomes an expression of the young people themselves. It is their offering to God. They offer their own thoughts and feelings. They use their own gifts and talents to enhance that offering.

If children participate in the planning and praying of the Mass, it will be an expression of their own life experiences. Unfortunately, children's liturgies are too often misnamed. Too frequently, they are the work of some well-intentioned adult. Most children's Masses are planned by adults. We, adults, do the work for the children, believing that the children will benefit from the experience.

Current literature provides sample Masses for teachers and liturgists. *Celebrations for Children*, *How Green Is Green*, *Liturgies for Children*, *On Cloud Nine* — all provide numerous Eucharistic celebrations. Indeed, these books are packaged liturgies "adaptable" to "any" group of children. But most are ideas and suggestions of adults for children. They express what adults think children want to say to God.

Purpose

The best resource for children's liturgies is the child. Children know best what will work for them and what they like. They need to participate in the planning and execution of their own prayer experiences for those experiences to be meaningful to them.

"...Liturgy is expressive human activity. The original Greek word for liturgy means 'the action of the people,' a meaning that suggests strongly that the people are expressing something by their action, that their action is expressive action. In its Christian sense, then, liturgy is an action by which a community bodies forth and expresses its attitude about the way it is between God and humankind, but more specifically about the way it is between this group gathered in the Spirit of Jesus and the one Jesus called Father. Quite simply, liturgy is a way of saying something" (Warren, 1977, p. 12).

How to Plan Children's Liturgies is an attempt to develop a resource for teachers and catechists to use in planning liturgies with children. Its aim is to find the prayer within the child. Children are the best resource.

The majority of educators in Catholic education are unsure of themselves in the field of religion. Witness the current emphasis on catechist and Master catechist training. The Church itself wishes to validate the qualifications of individuals for the teaching of religion. Workshops and in-services for the Catholic educator in the field of religion abound.

In *Sharing the Light of Faith*, Catholic Bishops said: "Teachers in Catholic schools are expected to accept and live the Christian message and to strive to instill a Christian spirit in their students. As catechists, they will meet standards equivalent to those set for other disciplines and possess the qualities described in Chapter IX, Part A" (p. 143). Each catechist is required to recognize his/her call from God to service, to live his/her faith, to believe in the Church, to share in the life of the Christian community, and to be committed to serving others.

If educators are "unsure" teaching religion, they are totally lost when it comes to preparing Eucharistic celebrations for or with their group of children. But teachers are ready learners. This is confirmed by Bruce Joyce and Beverly Showers (1980):

"The first message from research is very positive: teachers are wonderful learners. Nearly all teachers can acquire new skills that 'fine tune' their competence. They can also learn a considerable repertoire of teaching strategies that are new to them" (p. 379). *How to Plan Children's Liturgies* is a step by step process for the Catholic teacher and catechist to follow. It is a suggested method for developing the spiritual life of children and their understanding for the parts of the Mass. It is written as daily lesson plans for the teacher and catechist. *How to Plan Children's Liturgies* follows the guidelines the Church has set for Masses with children. It is written as a teacher's guide for planning Masses for children according to Church guidelines.

Methodology

For four years, I used a number of teaching techniques to encourage student participation in planning prayer services and liturgies. Successful planning seemed to result when one technique was used throughout planning sessions for any one prayer celebration. So I chose the technique that elicited the best response from my group. (See "Lesson Planning," page 8.) This technique was used and developed for three years.

During the fifth year of involvement in planning prayer services, other staff members asked for suggestions for how to involve students in planning sessions for prayer celebrations. As a result of several inquiries, I developed a rough draft of the lessons presented in the chapter titled "How to Plan Children's Liturgies." This was put together in 1979.

Because of growing interest in this field, three California Diocesan Educational offices requested that I present my ideas in a workshop for teachers of each of the three dioceses. The workshop, titled "How to Plan Children's Liturgies," was also presented in one segment of an educational television series. And I used the materials throughout two school years at Our Lady of the Rosary School in Union City, California. I further refined the lessons as a result of feedback from the workshop participants and student input during the school years 1980-1982.

Delineation of Study

The lessons presented in Chapter II are directed to educators of children in the primary grades, Kindergarten through third grade.

Children at this age-level are concrete learners. They do not abstract well. The average primary-aged child needs direction and guidance from the catechist.

Older children can be divided into committees to complete the various tasks for planning the parts of the Mass. Younger children require more supervision. In planning prayer services, young children work best as one large committee or committee of the whole. This enhances their over-all understanding of the liturgy and provides them with a better view of how the liturgy will progress.

The lessons in Chapter II are directed to teachers, parents and clergy who are working with primary-aged children to plan Masses with those children. Provision is made in the lessons for programs which meet daily as well as for those which meet weekly. The lessons suggest one method to use with children.

Organization of Remainder of Study

Chapter II contains the manuscript, "How to Plan Children's Liturgies." This material provides educators with a procedure to follow when working with children to plan and participate in children's liturgies. The work begins with some background for the educator. A section on why we pray and a brief overview complete aspects of the Mass that are important to the educator to know prior to his/her meeting with the children. The section titled "How to Use this Book" begins the clear, step by step process of planning with children. The rest is self-explanatory. Each section is explained separately.

Chapter III contains conclusions and recommendations for further study. As an educator, I was interested in providing an aid to other Catholic educators. As a Catholic, I wished to present children with a channel for them to express their prayer life in a meaningful way at communal celebrations. Chapter IV explores these two areas in relation to the material presented. It also offers some suggestions for further research in this area.

Chapter IV reviews literature in the field of children's liturgy. Included in this review are Roman Catholic Church documents relating to liturgy as well as a survey of resources that pertain to liturgy planning with children. The *Directory for Masses with Children*, a Church document published in 1973, opened the door for writers in this field. Prior to this time, children were not addressed by Church documents. As a result, the bulk of texts surveyed were published after 1973.

The Appendix contains material that you are free to copy if you have purchased the book. There are references in Chapter II to the appendix material.

How to Plan Children's Liturgies

This liturgy book is written as an aid to parents, teachers, catechists, and clergy in planning Eucharistic celebrations with children. The primary goal of this work is to make each celebration more child-like by using the children themselves as a primary resource. Make use of young people's words, thoughts, stories, drawings and prayers, and you will have a prayer experience that your group can identify as their own.

Children make mistakes. Do not expect a perfect work. But with your guidance, the youngsters will come to regard the Mass as an opportunity to express their needs to the Lord in their own language. They will be thankful to you for enabling them to love God in their own way, and to tell Him so. Children will be children. Help them to express themselves in appropriate ways.

By following some simple guidelines, you should be able to involve all of your children in the planning and prayer experience of the Mass. Begin your faith experiences at a level your children can understand. Then you will be able to gradually increase their appreciation and knowledge of the Mass. Incorporating activities from their religious education will help the children realize that the Mass is an important part of their spiritual life. It is not an isolated experience. Remember, you have the greatest resource in your own group of children.

I. Why Do We Pray?

The Mass is a celebration of the Lord among us. Each time you celebrate the Mass with your group of children, remind them of the reasons we pray. God calls to us; and we respond through prayer. Prayer is our opportunity to talk to God. We go to Him when we are happy and when we are sad.

Youngsters can best understand their relation with God on the level of need. We need God for our friend. He is all-knowing and all-wise. If we go to Him, we need to know that He will listen and help us. Tell a story or use a puppet to get the idea across to the children. Use the technique most suitable to your talent.

Here is a sample story: My friend Adrienne is moving to a new city. She is very worried. She has lived in Stockton all her life. She knows lots and lots of people there. And she is afraid that she will not be able to make new friends. She is nine years old. Finally, Adrienne got so worried that she started to cry. Crying did not help solve her problem. So she went to talk it over with her dad. He always seemed to be able to help her when she needed advice.

Adrienne's dad listened to her story. He smiled because he loved her so much. He said, "You will make friends, Adrienne. And I will help you. I can not make others like you. But I can tell you what to do so they will like you. Smile! Be friendly! Ask them about their city. Share your things. Can you do that?" Adrienne nodded her head. She had some ideas now about how she could make some new friends.

Here is a sample puppet skit: *Beaver*: "Boo Hoo...Boo Hoo...Oh what am I going to do? Wa...(Sob! Sob!) Oh, boys and girls, I am so upset. I have been trying to build a dam across the stream for two days, and I just can not do it. (Sob! Sob!) I know, I will ask Lion for some advice! Hey, Lion! Oh, Lion!" *Lion*: "Well, hel-lo Beaver. What is up? You have not come to see me for a visit in a long time!" *Beaver*: "I have this problem, Lion. I can not build the dam this year. The stream is too full. I almost make it, and then the water rushes past and knocks down all my work." *Lion* "Gee, I would like to help you, Beaver, but I do not swim myself! Say, have you thought of asking your neighbors, Mr. and Mrs. Duck? They are good swimmers. And they can help you carry sticks to your dam." *Beaver*: "That is a terrific idea. Thanks, Lion! See you later. I have lots to do. Bye!" *Lion*: "Bye, Beaver. Come again soon!"

Tell the children that we are often like Adrienne and Beaver. Problems come into our lives. We worry and fret and sometimes we cry because we are so upset. We need a friend to talk to. The best friend a person can have is God. He will always listen to us. And He will always help us with our troubles. He doesn't take away the problem, but He shows us what to do about it.

Explain that together you and the children will be planning a Mass celebration. You are going to go to God's house. And you will have the opportunity to talk to God about all your cares and worries. And God will give you some good advice to help you solve your difficulties.

II. Overview of the Mass

Discuss friendships with the children. Talk about their relationships with one another. Help them to recognize their need for others, for friends. The Mass is the best way for us to develop a friendship with God.

Explain the Mass in terms of a friendship. The Mass has three basic elements of friendship: communication, gift giving and communion. Ask the children how they know a friend. How do you know when you have a good friend? A friend shares, invites you to his/her house. A good friend stays with you no matter what. God does all this for us. He invites us to a celebration with all of His friends. We go to the Church and meet lots of people we know. Then we share. First we let God share with us. He tells us how to get to His home in Heaven. (Epistle and Gospel) Then we talk to Him. We share all our worries and cares. (Prayers of the Faithful) All this is communication.

Next, we give gifts to God. He gives us good health. He give us the air we breathe and everything in the world around us. At Mass we give back to Him the things that are important to us. You can tell the children that it is a bit like Christmas. You give and receive gifts with friends. God gives us His best gift, His Son, Jesus Christ, to be our friend in Communion.

Communion is the best part of a friendship. When you really know someone, you know what they like and do not like. Ask the children if they have ever had a friend who knew them really well, so well their friend seemed to know what they were thinking. Communion is like that. It is two in a union. We are in union with Jesus. It happens in a very visual way at Communion time. We eat the bread which has been changed to Christ's body. And we drink the wine which has been changed to Christ's blood. The bread, which is Christ, becomes a part of us; and we become a part of Christ. He is the vine and we are the branches. The most important celebration of our life together in Christ is the Mass.

Another way to present the Mass to children is in terms of a party. Your Mass will be a celebration, a party for all of God's favorite people, His children.

Compare the Mass to a party. Ask the children what they must do to plan a party. List all of the children's suggestions on the chalk board. Guide the group to suggest invitations, gifts, decorations, songs, activities, and speeches. Tell the children that in the Mass, we invite those we wish to attend. We decorate the Church for a party. We choose good songs to sing together. We bring bread and wine as gifts. We have speeches. We listen to God speak to us through the readings. A priest or guest speaker talks to us. Sometimes he leads us in talking to God. He might tell us some good things to do so we can talk better to Our Lord.

The Mass is a time to get to know God better. We are in His house. He listens to us and we listen to Him. Good friends begin to say and do things alike. As we become good friends with God, we say and do things as He would. The Mass is the best opportunity we have to get in touch with God and to have Him touch us.

III. How to Use This Book

Your first liturgy experience with the children is one of new beginnings. Since you will want this experience to occur as soon as possible toward the initial meetings of your group, you will be responsible for most of its organization. Then, as the year progresses, you can involve the children more and more in the planning. The children will learn more and more about the Mass as their involvement increases. You guide, but they choose. They will learn from you and from their mistakes. In this way, the Mass will come to mean something very special to them. Your goal will be to involve every child in some important way.

The following pages include progressive explanations of the various parts of the Mass. Once you understand the structure of the Mass and the method suggested, you will be able to use your own children as your best resource for planning Masses suited to their prayer life.

Try to make your first celebration as simple as possible. Remember, you are only beginning to raise the consciousness level of your group. This first faith experience should not be so deep as to confound the children. It should capture their attention and increase their desire to know more about this type of prayer.

IV. Lesson Planning

It is helpful to the youngsters if you follow the same pattern in your presentations in preparation for the Mass. Introduce each planning session with an object lesson. This will get the participants' attention. There are many resources available to you if you have difficulty coming up with your own lessons. Some include: *Little Threads* by Harvey D. and Patsie A. Moore, *61 Worship Talks for Children* by Eldon Weisheit, and *Bible Object Talks with Paper and Scissors* by Francis Clark Brown.

After you have the group's attention, review the part of the Mass you will be working on during that particular session. Make sure everyone understands exactly what you are doing.

Ask everyone for ideas. Get as many suggestions as you can. At this stage, all ideas are accepted. You are brainstorming. These ideas should be written down or tape recorded.

What is most important is to choose things that will help make your celebration a product of the children's ingenuity and creativity. You need to be realistic too. Evaluate each idea in terms of time and available resources. Choose the most practical for your group. Let the children have some part in the final decision-making.

V. Parts of the Mass

The Mass has many parts. Focusing the youngsters' attention on one or two at a time will better help them to understand what is taking place and why. Before you begin working on the various parts of the Mass, remind the children why we celebrate. We want to show that we are God's friends. Then, review the "Overview of the Mass" presented earlier in this chapter. Present an object lesson or puppet skit that demonstrates the need for everyone to help in the planning of the Mass.

Here is a sample skit:

Wolf: "Huff one...puff twice...huff one."
Teacher: "Hel-lo, Wolf! What are you doing here? Practicing for something?"
Wolf: "Oh, hi! Practicing? Yes, I'm going to enter the yoga body building class in my neighborhood. Say, there is something on my mind. Do you have time to help me?"
Teacher: "I'd sure like to, Wolf. What's the problem?"
Wolf: I have three friends. They really are in trouble.

They were thrown out of their apartment. And they
decided to build their own houses. And..."

Teacher: "I hope you are not going to ask me to build
three houses, Wolf!"

Wolf: "Oh, no! I wouldn't do that! No, they asked me
to help them. And I said, 'Yes!' But I found out that they
didn't ask anyone else. Just me! I can't carry all those
bricks. They weigh a ton! One of them even masked me how
wide to build a chimney. What am I going to do?"

Complete the skit spontaneously with your children. Their suggestions should lead them to understand that wolf cannot work alone. He needs help!

Here is a sample object lesson: Ask, "Will someone volunteer to take a few items to the office?" Choose one volunteer. Then, give the volunteer six or seven large, awkward items to carry.

Say, "It looks like our volunteer cannot do the job. Does anyone have any ideas to help get these items to the office?" Lead the children to suggest more helpers.

You need to stress the point that if the Mass is to be a product of the group, everyone must help. Wolf could not do it alone. We all need friends to help us.

With young children you cannot go into an indepth discussion on the parts of the liturgy. They will know certain parts and have questions about others. Take time to explain any part they seem to be unclear about.

VI. Theme

The basic question that youngsters ask about a Mass celebration is "What are we doing here?" or "Why do we have to go to Church?" It is a useful technique to put this question to the children. The presider or commentator can use it at the celebration to focus the children's attention on what is happening and what will happen next. Before the Theme explanation in the sample liturgies, such a question is stated. This is done for each part of the Mass. A question is asked to focus attention.

With primary-aged children, begin the discussion of theme with a role-playing situation. Pretend that Jesus has just walked into the room. Give as many boys and girls as possible an opportunity to say what they would ask Jesus to help them with if He was sitting in the room. Use a cloud or picture of fire or some other symbol and label it *God*. Let the children address the symbol expressing their concerns.

After the role-playing session, kindergarteners and first graders can draw on a piece of paper the things they want God to help them with. Aides or older children may assist by writing down what a particular picture means to each artist.

For second and third graders, make a ditto using the correct format for writing a letter. Review the format with the children. Tell them to write to God asking for His special help or telling Him about something wonderful that might have happened.

After class, read the letters or review the pictures. Put them into groups according to content. You will see ideas repeat and overlap. Select three or four that are mentioned most frequently.

At your next meeting, list the topics chosen on the chalk board. For the younger children, you can use a symbol to represent each theme. Next, under each topic, list the needs as the children volunteer responses. What will you pray for under each category? If the theme is "Family," then you might pray that all have good health, and that all are happy. These are our needs, the things we ask God to give us. But there is more to our theme planning.

Explain that liturgy is a covenant with God. In child-like terms, covenant means a two-sided promise. I promise God and He promises me. We must keep our part of the promise just as God keeps His part. The stories about Adrienne and Beaver at the beginning of the chapter illustrated this. Both Adrienne and Beaver needed help to solve their problems, but they had to do something too.

Further explain to the children that from the very beginning, God and His people made promises to each other. He promises to take care of us if we listen to His words. If we ask God to take care of our families, what is our side of the bargain? What could we do? Typical responses might include doing chores and not talking back.

List all responses underneath the appropriate theme suggestions. Your board might look something like the example on page 54.

The promise is two-sided. God will help, but the *US* tells the children what they agree to do.

After going through this process of selection for a theme, your group will realize that whatever topic is chosen, they will have to make a conscious response to do something about their part of the promise. Give the children a little time to decide which idea will be the one they will use for a theme. Ask the youngsters to vote for one. A hand vote is sufficient.

Write a short explanation of this decision-making process for the "Theme" at the beginning of your liturgy. Be sure to include some of the children's own thoughts. Here are some samples:

"We are beginning a new school year. Today we are celebrating all the things God helps us to do, see, feel, hear, talk and so much more. God gives us many gifts and we hope to learn to use them."

"Today we thank God for the beautiful earth. Please help us to respect nature and life, and to use all the resources you give us correctly. We will be kind and share with one another and help each other when we are sad. We will try to keep our school clean and be careful not to step on plants."

"We are here today to pray for peace all around the world. We ask God to prevent nuclear war and to help people so that they stay in good health. We promise to set a good example for everyone, to be kind, and to pray for others."

After the final selection, ask everyone to make a pencil drawing expressing his/her idea of the theme. These drawings will be very useful for illustrations in the Mass booklet, for banner making, invitations and slide photographs.

VII. Theme Development

You should plan activities that will reinforce your group's understanding of the theme they have chosen. You want to broaden their perspective, and give them an opportunity to more deeply appreciate their choice. Follow the format of the student's text for Religion to develop a typical session supporting your chosen theme.

Some lesson ideas to develop a theme of "Saints" might include:

1. Bring some short stories to class about different saints. Read the stories and talk about the things that make a person holy.

2. Bring to class pictures of people living today who are saints. (Mother Teresa of Calcutta and Dom Helder Camara) Ask, "What does it mean to be a saint?"

3. Invite a grandparent to class. Ask the visitor to talk about the saints. Let the grandparent share what he/she has done to lead a good life.

4. Take the children to your Church. Is it named after or dedicated to a saint? Are there statues of different saints in it? Are there saints in the stained glass windows? Talk about the saints, especially the patron of the parish or diocese.

5. Teach a song about the saints. "I Sing a Song of the Saints of God" or "When the Saints Go Marchin' In" are good examples.

6. We can all become saints. Saints are holy people. They are people who do what God wants them to do. Sometimes it is not easy, but it is important to try. Jesus is an example for us. He was good and kind. He taught us that we are all God's children. God is our Father. And He has a place for us in Heaven. "We are now God's children." (1 John 3:2) Talk about this with the group.

7. We have a special book to help us to know the right things to do. God has His words for us in the Bible. By listening to scripture readings, we will know what God has in mind for us. God sent His Son Jesus to help us. If we can be more like Him, we will be doing the kinds of things that God wants us to do. Share stories from the *New Testament* that demonstrate how Jesus wants us to behave.

8. Make a mural. Write the words, "Friends of God," at the top of a large sheet of butcher paper. Let all of the boys and girls draw themselves and print their names on it.

9. As a group, write a prayer asking God to help you to be more like the saints.

10. Direct the children to role-play some everyday experiences. Ask, "How do you think a saint would behave lining up? Getting a drink? Sharpening pencils? Playing a game? Meeting someone in trouble? Seeing paper on the ground in the school yard?"

11. For homework tonight, surprise your parents by doing everything they ask you to do. Be a saint!

Library books provide an excellent resource for developing themes. You might find books of ditto masters and object lessons on various topics. After giving more time to developing the theme, you and the youngsters will be better prepared to celebrate the Mass. Use the worksheet on page 55 for Theme Development.

VIII. Invitations

Ask the children who they would like to invite to the Mass you are planning. At a Mass for All Saints' Day a group chose to invite their grandparents. They felt that their grandmas and grandpas were more like saints than anyone else. The list should include a presider, principal of your program, Religion coordinator, and other grades in the school or catechetical program, unless it is a small group Mass.

Let the boys and girls decide how they will invite their guests. If they want to send written invitations, they might use the same drawing that will be used for the cover of the Mass booklet. Let the children choose one drawing from the ones they did to illustrate the theme. Copy it on a ditto master. Make an invitation by writing the words, "You are invited to a special Mass celebrating...*(Explain your theme here!)*. Time:_____ Place:_____ Date:_____ Please come! Love, Grade_____." See pages 56 and 57 for examples.

Confirm date, time and place of the Mass with the celebrant. Include this information on the invitation. Make enough copies for all those to be invited. Ask the children to color the invitations. And choose children to deliver them.

The children might decide to write personal invitations or to go visit those they wish to attend and ask them in person. These are acceptable alternatives. Inviters need encouragement and reminders

After the celebration of the Mass, it would be appropriate to send "Thank you" notes or some of the children's drawings to the presider, homilist and guests. Make a list of those you need to thank and divide the group accordingly.

IX. Mass Booklet

The Mass booklet will take some time to put together. What is important is that the children have something to follow so they can keep up with what is happening and fully participate.

The booklet is a teaching tool. The cover may have art extending over a two page spread, front and back cover. The children can color their own and share their feelings about the picture in relation to the theme they have chosen for the Mass. They can put their names on their Mass booklets. Either by themselves, or with an aide or older student, they can write a story relating to the theme on the inside of the cover. Also, having booklets to color will keep many hands busy while you practice with readers and those in the Offertory Procession.

X. General Guidelines for Typing the Mass Booklet

Follow the outline on page 14 as you type the parts of the Mass. Type all people parts in capital letters, and celebrant parts in lower case. Use block letters for the words on the cover. And introduce each part of the Mass with Italic writing, primary printing or handwriting. This helps to focus attention on each part of the Mass.

Type all words to songs that you want everyone to sing. Be sure to obtain the necessary permissions. Include the Eucharistic Prayer you will be using, especially if it has responses throughout.

If you have access to a copier, type all materials with a carbon ribbon on white paper. If you are typing on ditto masters, you can type straight onto the dittos for a booklet 8½" × 11" or divide the masters in half prior to typing, with a felt tip marker. Type the liturgy. You may need to cut the dittos apart and reattach them so they are in proper sequence.

Four pages will produce a booklet 8½" × 5½" when folded in half. If your book is five or six pages, use the back of the cover for printing. This will conserve paper. An eight or nine page booklet might look like this:

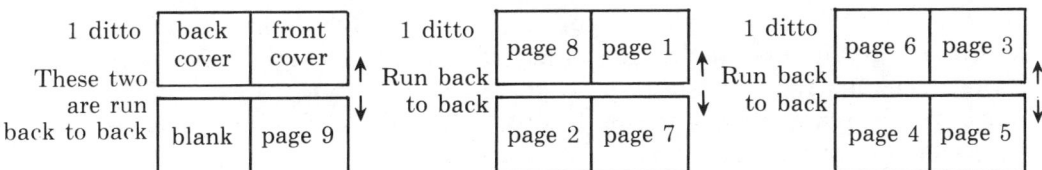

Use the drawings from the Theme session to illustrate the booklet. Trace the children's pictures onto the pages. Be sure to number the pages.

Do the cover ahead of time. This will give you an opportunity to use it in a session for Theme development. It, too, should be one of the youngsters' art. Let the boys and girls choose which drawing to use.

Give the music leader, principal and other teachers copies ahead of time. Ask for volunteers to pass out booklets at the beginning of the Mass. When other classes or groups of children are invited, get their booklets to their teachers early so they can practice too.

Use a felt tip marker to highlight special parts for readers, or anyone else who has some assignment during the Mass. It will help each participant know when to do his part. Highlight a booklet for the celebrant and go over it with him. Invite him to come to one of your planning sessions and talk to the group on the theme selected.

XI. Timeline

To facilitate planning a Mass with children, develop a timeline. Decide which parts of the Mass to illuminate for the boys and girls. Each of your celebrations should help them to understand this form of worship to a greater degree.

Consider first the essentials. According to the *Directory for Masses With Children* (1974),

The general structure of the Mass, which 'in some sense consists of two parts, namely, the liturgy of the word and the liturgy of the eucharist,' should always be maintained as should some rites to open and conclude the celebration" (Paragraph 38). Adaptations to aid the learning processes of the youngsters are admissible with the following limitations: The introductory rites should include some explanation of the theme, and one other element plus a concluding prayer. No part should be entirely neglected at all of your celebrations (Paragraph 40).

At the liturgy of the word, the reading of the Gospel must always be included (Paragraphs 41-49). In the liturgy of the eucharist, the eucharistic prayer is of greatest importance (Paragraphs 50-52). "At the end of the eucharistic prayer, the Lord's Prayer, the breaking of bread, and the invitation to communion should always follow" (Paragraph 53).

In the closing rites, the invitation which precedes the final blessing is important. The *Directory* encourages richer forms of blessing, but the trinitarian formula with the sign of the cross should conclude the Mass (Paragraph 54).

These are the essentials (see Appendix on page 50). Choose other parts to develop along with these, and you are ready to make a timeline. The ideal is a separate session for each part of the Mass you wish to work on. If time is limited, however, you might have to do more than one element in a given session. If time is really short, you might have to make some decisions for the children. Remember, the more they decide, the more a children's liturgy you will have. Do not forget time to type the booklet and time to practice with the children.

Here is an outline of the parts of the Mass. Starred (*) elements should never be omitted.

I. Opening Rites
  *A. Theme
  B. Hymn
  C. Procession
  D. Greeting
  E. Penitential Rite
  F. Gloria
  *G. Collect (Opening Prayer)

II. Liturgy of the Word
  A. Old Testament Reading
  B. Responsorial Psalm
  C. New Testament Reading
  D. Alleluia verse
  *E. Gospel
  F. Homily
  G. Creed
  H. Prayers of the Faithful

III. Liturgy of the Eucharist
  A. Preparation of the Gifts
    1. Song
    2. Offertory Procession

*B. Eucharistic Prayer
  *1. Proclamation of the Mystery of Faith
  *2. Amen
C. Communion Rite
  *1. Our Father
  2. Sign of Peace
  *3. Breaking of the Bread
  4. Prayer
  *5. Invitation to Communion
  *6. Communion
  7. Communion Hymn
  8. Communion Meditation
  9. Post Communion Prayer

IV. Closing Rites
  A. Announcements
  *B. Invitation
  *C. Blessing
  D. Dismissal
  E. Closing Song

Choose elements from each of the four major sections of the Mass to develop with the children. No part should be neglected from all of your celebrations.

Now you are ready to develop a timeline for your work with the children. A sample timeline for a five-day-a-week program might look like this:

FIRST WEEK
    Monday: Mass overview
    Tuesday: Theme
    Wednesday: Theme development
    Thursday: Decorations
    Friday: Songs

SECOND WEEK
    Monday: Invitations
    Tuesday: Readings and Response
    Wednesday: Prayers
    Thursday: Prayers of the Faithful
    Friday: Offertory Procession

THIRD WEEK
    Monday: Eucharistic Prayer
    Tuesday: Blessing
    Wednesday: Type Mass booklet and print copies
    Thursday: Meet with celebrant, practice songs and special parts
    Friday: Servers and ushers

FOURTH WEEK
    Monday: Celebrant presents lesson to group
    Tuesday: Practice
    Wednesday: Practice
    Thursday: Practice

Friday: Mass

If your program meets only once a week, your timeline might look like this:

FIRST MASS
First Meeting: Mass overview
Second Meeting: Theme, Theme development
Third Meeting: Decorations, Invitations
Fourth Meeting: Readings, Songs,
Mass

SECOND MASS
First Meeting: Theme, Theme development
Second Meeting: Decorations, Invitations
Third Meeting: Readings, Songs
Fourth Meeting: Prayers of the Faithful, Offertory Procession
Mass

THIRD MASS
First Meeting: Theme, Decorations
Second Meeting: Songs, Readings
Third Meeting: Creed, Sign of Peace
Fourth Meeting: Eucharistic Prayer
Mass

FOURTH MASS
First Meeting: Theme, Gloria
Second Meeting: Readings, Homily
Third Meeting: Songs, Our Father
Fourth Meeting: People responses, Prayers
Mass

Try to vary the parts of the Mass your group will illuminate at the different celebrations you share and plan together. This way, you will not omit any part at all your celebrations. And the children will come to understand the importance and significance of each part.

XII. Decorations

Celebration includes decoration. Think of birthday parties, anniversaries, Christmas and Thanksgiving celebrations. What we choose for ornamentation usually tells everyone who is invited or who happens to walk by that something special is happening. Children enjoy this part of Mass planning because they love to decorate.

Begin the planning session with an object lesson focused on the theme of the Mass. Try a little magic with a *Fun Magic Coloring Book* (Fun Incorporated, 1977 Chicago, Illinois 60614). Show the blank coloring book. Ask the group to think of drawings on the theme of magic. Use some magic dust (it is invisible!). And show the black line drawings in the coloring book. Ask the group to think of their favorite color. Once again sprinkle magic dust and show colored drawings. Later — invite the children to make a drawing on their theme. If the decorations reflect the theme, they can be used in theme development lessons and also in the homily.

everyone who participates what you are celebrating. Then, begin brainstorming ideas with the group.

Write the youngsters' suggestions on the chalk board. Here are sample results from primary-aged groups using the theme of Thanksgiving:

KINDERGARTEN
1. Make a giant scarecrow. Put "thank you" cards in his
pockets to be distributed during mass.
2. Make a banner saying, "Happy Thanksgiving!"
3. Make Indian and pilgrim hats and wear them to Church.
Do not forget to make one for our giant scarecrow.

FIRST GRADE
1. Make huge pumpkins for altar decorations. Add eyes,
noses and mouths (features) during the Offertory Procession,
and thank God for use of our five senses during the prayers.
2. Draw pictures of things we are thankful for.
Enlarge the pictures and color. Use these to decorate
the pews.

SECOND GRADE
1. Make a cardboard Mayflower boat for an altar banner.
2. Dress up like members of the Mayflower crew.
3. Bring up offertory gifts that represent the many countries
our forefathers came from.

THIRD GRADE
1. Bring pictures of people and things we are thankful for.
Make collages.
2. Paint a mural of the first Thanksgiving.
3. Buy helium balloons. Put names of things we are thankful
for on them. Place them on the pews and release them after
Mass.

After you have collected all the ideas you can from the children, choose the practical. The boys and girls will understand when you tell them why one or another idea cannot be done. Available materials and time will play big roles in your decision-making. Be positive in your approach. Once you have indicated the possible options, let the children make the final selection. Remember, your goals are to make the celebration a product of the youngsters' ingenuity and creativity, and to help make their ideas successful.

You aid the children first by process. Begin making the decorations as soon as possible in your preparations for the Mass. Depending on what your group finally decides to make, you may find it easier to work in small groups, individually or all together. Decide what is best for your group of children.

Next, you need to consider the choices of the children and the most expedient method of executing their ideas. You know your group, their talents and gifts. You know what they can and cannot do. Here are some suggestions for different types of decorations.

Banners

Use "Theme" illustration drawings (p. 9). Place a transparency on top of the pictures you wish to enlarge. Trace the drawings. Next, place the transparency on the overhead projector and enlarge the picture on butcher paper. Use an opaque projector to produce the same results. Add color with paint, crayon, or magic markers. For quick results, take the markers apart. The ink strip works like a huge brush.

Cloth Banners

Use the children's art work and enlarge it using the process explained above. Collect pieces of material. Make the first enlargement on butcher paper. Cut it apart and use the pieces for patterns. Stitch-witchery will "glue" the material faster than sewing it. All you need is a hot iron. Remember to use caution with this appliance.

Faces Without Features

Youngsters' drawings of people faces or pumpkins are enlarged. Features are made separately. During the entrance procession of the Mass, a group of boys and girls add the features to the faces already hung in place. These would include eyes, noses, mouths and ears. Place a small "x" on each spot on each face where each feature is to be placed. Be sure to let the children practice ahead of time!

Banners With Words

If a message is important enough to be displayed, it should be readable. Show the group different thicknesses of letters from a distance. Block letters are most effective. Another technique is to use small drawings to make up letters. Each boy and girl could be asked to trace their hands, or draw "palm-sized" pumpkins. Any symbol that might express the theme could be used. These would then be cut out, colored and placed together to spell the words to be used such as "Happy Thanksgiving!" This encourages a closer look before and after the celebration of the Mass by all participating.

The children should also recognize the importance of contrast. Blues, browns and reds will not show up on a dark wood background. If a poster is drawn on white poster paper, color the background with the side of a crayon. This will cut the stark contrast of color verses white.

Large Single Item

The group might choose to make six to eight large items such as pumpkins or horns of plenty or a combination of two symbols. Enlarge these as directed earlier and let the children color them working in groups. The impact of single items can be quite impressive. Saints can be drawn easily be tracing the bodies of the children on butcher paper. For a May Crowning Mass you might choose to draw flowers and enlarge them. (The radius of each flower should be about 12" to 15".) Give the boys and girls large sheets of fadeless paper, butcher paper or wallpaper pages from sample wallpaper books. Use green fadeless paper for stems and leaves. The flowers, when completed, should be close to six feet tall to create the desired effect.

Almost any item is enlargeable. Encourage the children to pick one that fits their theme. The group might choose to enlarge different symbols. For the feast of the Immaculate Conception, one third grade class decided to enlarge six different symbols for Mary: a chair (Seat of Wisdom), a gate (Gate of Heaven), a star (Morning Star), a house (House of Gold), a tower (Tower of David), and a rose (Mystical Rose). Each symbol represented a title of Mary's. They also cut out block letters and placed these around the symbols. Our pastor changed the English titles to Spanish and used the decorations for the feast of Our Lady of Guadalupe.

The above examples indicate how decorations may be used to highlight the celebration of the Eucharist. This list is not the last word on ideas. You will find that one idea leads to another. Do not forget to include decorations that relate life experiences to faith celebrations. Also, do not hesitate to use simple line drawings that are meaningful to the children. Simply ask permission of the artist to put a label on the work. Everyone will know what the artist intended.

The children's art will enhance the celebration of the Mass. It will provide a bridge for further theme development both prior to and during the Mass. It can also be used after the Mass for decorating the meeting place. Most decorations are time consuming to make. They are, however, worthwhile. Be sure to allow plenty of time to make the items your boys and girls choose. And remember too, it takes time to display the work.

XIII. Songs

Mass is a celebration. We sing when we are happy. Begin this session by playing some current song or song from the children's catechetical program. Ask what the message of the song is. What are the writers of the song trying to tell us about God or about His creation?

Teach a simple round song to the youngsters. You might use puppets: *Teacher*: "Dolores, where are you?" *Dolores*: "I'm right here!" *Teacher*: "I hope you are feeling O.K. today?" *Dolores*: "If you mean can I sing, I only promise to try." *Teacher*: "Do you know the tune to 'Frere Jacques'?" *Dolores*: "...hmmm..." (Hums the tune!) *Teacher*: "Good! The words are, 'Alleluia' and 'Praise the Lord.'" *Dolores*: "Alleluia, Praise the Lord!" *Teacher*: "Let's try it together. (Sing song.) Thank you, Dolores!" *Dolores*: "Anytime! Bye!"

There are many ways to present songs and many places to sing in the Mass. The boys and girls might ask the congregation to greet the celebrant with the opening song, a small group to sing an offertory hymn, and a soloist to sing the communion song. Songs with gestures might be an appropriate response to the readings. Use the illustration on page 58 of the Appendix to explain all the possibilities to the group.

Begin by asking the children to suggest songs that relate to the theme they have chosen. Check with your music leader or a parent with musical ability. These resource people can provide insight and help teach new songs.

Use resource material and supplementary materials. Go through song books ahead of time so that you can present new songs to the group. Perhaps a boy or girl in your group plays the piano or some other musical instrument. They may have some unique suggestions.

Consider gestures done by mirroring of the teacher or leader by the children. The group might say the Lord's Prayer together as they follow the leader's movements. You might want the group to stand together on the altar steps for this prayer. This technique is especially good for teachers who are not strong singers. Hap Palmer records provide good background for gestures.

The *Directory for Masses With Children* encourages the use of musical instruments. If you have children with special talents, the Mass is the perfect opportunity for them to share their gifts with others. It is easy to find out if someone is gifted in this way. Otherwise, someone may volunteer when encouraged.

After the brainstorming session with the children, decide as a group when you want to sing. Possibilities include:

entrance _____
Gloria _____
Response to readings _____
alleluia verse _____
offertory _____
responses to Eucharistic prayers _____
Acclamation _____
Amen _____
Our Father _____
sign of peace _____
Lamb of God _____
communion 1. _____
                2. _____
communion meditation _____
blessing _____
closing _____

Choose appropriate songs. Decide on a form for presentation. One person, a small group, or the entire congregation might be asked to sing each song. Consider also whether to use gestures, instruments or professional recordings (records or cassettes). Choral reading too is an option. The children may want to vary the presentation of songs or to use the same format throughout. They might want quiet time with no music or singing. Be sure to make them aware of the possibilities.

Song is a communal response. It does provide a forum for expressing peoples' feelings. With your help, the children will see or begin to see the truth in the songs and ponder aspects in their own lives that relate to them.

XIV. People Responses

As you begin to discuss the various parts of the Mass with your group of children, you will discover that there are certain parts of the Mass that the children are very familiar with. One aspect frequently overlooked in preparing for a Mass with young people is review of the traditional responses the congregation says at Mass.

You might explain to the children that at the celebration of the Mass our words and actions are an expression of our unity. The Mass is a communal celebration. We pray as a community. So everyone's participation in action and word is a sign of our life together in Christ. We form one body, the Church. Encourage participation by reviewing the traditional responses. This can be done at the final practice with your group or review parts at each of your planning sessions. Choose different responses to emphasize at each of your Mass celebrations.

The responses include:

AT THE GREETING

Father: The grace of our Lord Jesus Christ and the love of God and the fellowship of the Holy Spirit be with all of you.

All: And also with you.

AT THE PENITENTIAL RITE

All: I confess to almighty God, and to you, my brothers and sisters, that I have sinned through my own fault in my thoughts and in my words, in what I have done, and in what I have failed to do; and I ask Blessed Mary, ever virgin, all the angels and saints, and you, my brothers and sisters, to pray for me to the Lord our God.

or Lord have mercy. Christ have mercy. Lord have mercy.

AT THE GLORIA

All: Glory to God in the highest, and peace to his people on earth. Lord, God, heavenly King, almighty God and Father, we worship you, we give you thanks, we praise you for your glory. Lord Jesus Christ, only Son of the Father, Lord God, Lamb of God, you take away the sin of the world: have mercy on us; you are seated at the right hand of the Father: receive our prayer. For you alone are the Holy One, you alone are the Lord, you alone are the Most High, Jesus Christ, with the Holy Spirit, in the glory of God the Father. Amen.

AFTER THE OPENING PRAYER

All: Amen.

AFTER THE FIRST READING

Reader: This is the word of the Lord.

All: Thanks be to God.

AFTER THE SECOND READING

Reader: This is the word of the Lord.

All: Thanks be to God.

AT THE READING OF THE GOSPEL

Father: Aleluia.

All: Alleluia

Father: (Scripture verse varies.)

All: Alleluia

Father: The Lord be with you.

All: And also with you.

Father: A reading from the holy Gospel according to (Matthew, Mark, Luke or John).

All: Glory to you, Lord.

AT THE CONCLUSION OF THE GOSPEL

Father: This is the Gospel of the Lord.

All: Praise to you, Lord Jesus Christ.

AFTER THE PRAYER WHICH ENDS THE PRAYER OF THE FAITHFUL

All: Amen.

AT THE PREPARATION OF THE GIFTS (IF THERE IS NO OFFERTORY SONG)

Father: Blessed are you, Lord, God of all creation. Through your goodness we have this bread to offer which earth has given and human hands have made. It will become for us the bread of life.

All: Blessed be God forever.

Father: Blessed are you, Lord, God of all creation. Through your goodness we have this wine to offer, fruit of the vine and work of human hands. It will become our spiritual drink.

All: Blessed be God forever.

AT THE PRAYER OVER THE GIFTS

Father: Pray, brethren, that our sacrifice may be acceptable to God, the almighty Father.

All: May the Lord accept the sacrifice at your hands for the praise and glory of His name, for our good and the good of all his Church.

Father: (Prayer varies.)

All: Amen.

AT THE BEGINNING OF THE EUCHARISTIC PRAYERS

Father: The Lord be with you.

All: And also with you.

Father: Lift up your hearts.

All: We lift them up to the Lord.

Father: Let us proclaim the mystery of faith:

All: Christ has died, Christ is risen, Christ will come again.

AFTER PREFACE

All: Holy, holy, holy Lord, God of power and might, Heaven and earth are full of your glory. Hosanna in the highest. Blessed is he who comes in the name of the Lord. Hosanna in the highest.

AT THE MYSTERY OF FAITH

Father: et us proclaim the mystery of faith:

All: Christ has died, Christ is risen, Christ will come again.

or Dying you destroyed our death, rising you restored our life, Lord Jesus, come in glory.

or When we eat this bread and drink this cup, we proclaim your death, Lord Jesus, until you come in glory.

or Lord, by your cross and resurrection you have set us free. You are the Savior of the world.

AT THE CONCLUSION OF THE EUCHARISTIC PRAYER

Father: Through him, with him, in him, in the unity of the Holy Spirit, all glory and honor is yours, almighty Father, for ever and ever.

All: Amen.

AT THE LORD'S PRAYER

Father: Let us pray with confidence to the Father in the words our Savior gave us.

All: Our Father, who art in heaven, hallowed be thy name; thy kingdom come; thy will be done on earth as it is in heaven. Give us this day our daily bread; and forgive us our trespasses as we forgive those who trespass against us; and lead us not into temptation, but deliver us from evil.

Father: Deliver us, Lord, from every evil, and grant us peace in our day. In your mercy keep us free from sin and protect us from all anxiety as we wait in joyful hope for the coming of our Savior, Jesus Christ.

All: For the kingdom, the power, and the glory are yours, now and for ever.

AT THE SIGN OF PEACE

Father: Lord, Jesus Christ, you said to your apostles: I leave you peace, my peace I give you. Look not on our sins, but on the faith of your Church, and grant us the peace and unity of your kingdom where you live for ever and ever.

All: Amen.

Father: The peace of the Lord be with you always.

All: And also with you.

AT THE BREAKING OF THE BREAD

All: Lamb of God, you take away the sins of the world: have mercy on us. Lamb of God, you take away the sins of the world: have mercy on us. Lamb of God, you take away the sins of the world: grant us peace.

AT COMMUNION

Father: This is the Lamb of God who takes away the sins of the world. Happy are those who are called to his supper.

All: Lord, I am not worthy to receive you, but only say the word and I shall be healed.

Father: The body of Christ.

Communicant: Amen.

PRAYER AFTER COMMUNION

Father: Let us pray. (Prayer varies.)

All: Amen.

CONCLUDING RITE

Father: The Lord be with you.
All: And also with you.
BLESSING
Father: May almighty God bless you, the Father, and the Son, and the Holy Spirit.
All: Amen.
DISMISSAL
Father: Go in the peace of Christ.
or The Mass is ended; go in peace.
or Go in peace to love and serve the Lord.
All: Thanks be to God.

These responses are presented on Appendix pages 70-74 in larger, reproducible print.

XV. Penitential Rite

The Introductory Rites of the Mass include a song, greeting by the priest, theme explanation, Penitential Rite, Gloria and opening prayer or Collect. Use page 59 of the Appendix to illustrate this. There should be a time when we really stop and talk about the fact that sometimes we hurt others. During the Mass, there is such an opportunity in the Penitential Rite. Jesus said that if we had some hurt involving someone, we should leave our gift at the altar and go and make up with that person. In the spirit of celebration, we want to make everything perfect and beautiful for our main guest, Jesus. Just as we dust and sweep and clean to ready our homes for a party, so a time is set aside to think of our failings and to ask God to forgive us. We ask God to help us personally to be ready for the coming of Jesus.

The Penitential prayers come from the children's experiences. They know what things they want to bring to God. The basic question is, "Why should we be sorry?" Let the group share areas of weakness, things they have done to hurt others or things they have failed to do. There are several lead questions you might use to stimulate discussion. What do you do that makes others feel sad or cry? Are you always as helpful and responsible as you should be? What kinds of things do you do that your Mom, Dad, or teacher do not like? How are we mean to our playmates and friends?

Choose three areas of concern that the boys and girls agree are true for most of them. Use these statements in the Penitential Rite of the Mass you are planning together. Some samples include:

For stealing
For being mean to other people
For talking back to our Moms and Dads
For breaking someone else's toys
For saying bad words
For cheating on our classwork and tests
For taking other people's things without asking
For not doing the things we are told to do

The response the congregation will make when the priest reads the three statements your group picks is "Lord have mercy, Christ have mercy, Lord have mercy."

End this session with the children by praying for forgiveness. Spontaneously join hands and ask God to forgive each member of your group. Plan a Penance Service or Rite of Reconciliation prior to the Mass you are planning. Include all of the suggestions made by the participants as an examination of conscience.

Being forgiven is one of the most beautiful aspects of being a Christian. God forgives us no matter what we do. It is important to impress the youngsters with this fact. Use the story of the Prodigal Son and other scripture stories to emphasize this for the children.

XVI Prayers

We pray because we believe God is here, present in our midst. The Mass is a shared prayer, a communal offering to the Father.

"Kneeling, genuflecting, standing and sitting are all good and necessary postures of prayer. Each provides one experience and expression of the soul's many-faceted relationship to God. And there are any number of other postures which have been or will be created to satisfy our longing to give meaningful form to our prayer, to offer our entire selves — body and soul — to God. The Church must offer her support and encouragement to us to pray as whole persons" (Deitering, 1980, pp. 37-38).

"The Church charges us who worship in a parish or a community to be a sign of unity. She encourages postures common to and shared by all as signs of unity in the faith." (Deitering, 1980, p. 38)

Begin your session on prayer with the children by praying with them. Ask them to stand and stretch together. Tell them to reach for the presence of God. Then ask them to sit, slowly and humbly in His presence. And finally, tell them to drop to one knee to tell God they will do His will. Say, "Tell God in your heart, that He is the Maker of the world and your God for ever and ever." Excellent resources for prayer experiences include: *Experiments in Prayer*; *Experiments in Growth*; *Actions, Gestures & Bodily Attitudes,* and *The Blessing Cup*. There are many books of this type available.

After you have shared a prayer experience with the group, let the participants share prayer experiences of their own, telling of different times when they felt particularly close to God. Guide them in writing three prayers, one for the Collect or opening of Mass, one for the conclusion of the Prayers of the Faithful, and one for after Communion, the Post Communion prayer.

The Collect is a special prayer which includes some concern as expressed in the theme of the Mass. Ask the group for suggestions for their favorite name for God. How do they address their God? Do they call Him Father? Do they feel more comfortable calling Him Lord? Let them tell you. Next, compose a sentence which describes God. "Father, You are the Savior of the world." "Almighty God, You are the creator of all." Again, accept the children's suggestions.

The third line of the prayer can relate to the theme. It might be expressed as petition or thanksgiving. "Help us to be at peace with each other." "Help us to do well in school." "Please, bring peace to Ireland and all the parts of the world." "Bless our animals and take care of them always." "Thank you for all the gifts you give us, especially our good health." Remind the children of the theme and ask for suggestions related to it.

The next line is one of praise. "Lord, you always listen to me when I need you." "Lord, you answer our needs daily." "God, we love you and will love you forever." Give some examples of praise if the group has trouble coming up with their own ideas. This will stimulate their thinking.

End all your prayers with the word, "Amen." It means, "Yes, I believe it. It is true." This word is a rich word in our religious tradition. In the Old Testament it was used to end prayers. In the New Testament, Jesus used it to precede his words. "Amen, amen I say to you..." he would frequently begin. It is an awakening word. We must be awake to our faith and belief in the Lord. Renew the life of this word with your group.

For the prayer at the conclusion of the Prayers of the Faithful, follow the instructions for the Collect except for the third line. Here, include one of the petitions used for the Prayers of the Faithful. "Answer our petitions especially our prayers for our parents." "Lord, listen to our prayers especially our needs for help in school." "Help us, Father, to do what our parents tell us to do." The children will have one area of need that stands out in their minds as needing extra attention. This gives them the opportunity to express it.

The Post Communion prayer follows the same format also with only one variation. This is the final formal prayer of the Mass. It provides an opportunity for the children to thank God for listening to their prayer and to unify the Mass. We end the Mass as we began it. We pray for the intention first mentioned in the theme and thank God for listening to all our prayers. The third line reflects these thoughts. "Thank you, God, for bringing peace to the world. Thank you for listening to our prayers." "Thank you, Lord, for helping us get along better with our brothers and sisters. You really help us when we ask You." "Thank you for animals. Thank you for taking care of them. Thank you for helping us to love and care for them." Read the completed prayer to the group. Get their final approval.

Use the chalk board or butcher paper as you and the boys and girls work on the prayers. Write their ideas down. If two suggestions are made, vote to find their favorite. Keep the prayers short. You want them to understand that prayer is part of their own lived experience, a part of their own lives. It should come from concerns and needs that are real to them. As they participate in composing prayers, they should begin to see that the prayers used at other Masses were written by real people too. And, hopefully, the message of the authors will take on some meaning in the lives of the children.

XVII. Readings

At the conclusion of the Introductory Rite, we begin the Liturgy of the Word, the listening, learning part of the celebration (see page 60 in the Appendix). We begin with a reading from the Old Testament. The Old Testament reading is a reminder of our roots and the beginning of salvation history in the Judeo-Christian tradition. The second reading is customarily from the New Testament letters of Paul, James, Peter, John and Jude. It is a call to the Christian life. The Gospel reading is the highpoint of the Liturgy of the Word. It is Jesus' life shared with us. It tells us what Jesus said and did during his lifetime. It is four accounts of his life, death, and resurrection from the dead. The four evangelists, Matthew, Mark, Luke and John, wrote of their own experiences with Jesus. And they share their faith experiences with us through their writing.

Before planning the readings with your group, do some research. Find several readings that relate to the theme your group has chosen. In place of an object lesson, find a filmstrip or movie that relates a Gospel story. Invite older students to come to your meeting and act out a story from the Bible. The greater importance you place on presenting the readings will certainly be reflected by your youngsters. Your enthusiasm will become their own.

Let the children themselves act out some of the stories. You read, and they mime. Use puppets to tell the story. Draw pictures to illustrate parts of the story and make slides. Let the children make up the narrative to accompany the slides. This way, the story becomes part of their own experience. And they begin to understand that scripture has meaning for us today. After an activity, the selection can be reread from scripture with an increased awareness and appreciation for the message.

Paragraphs 41 through 47 in the *Directory for Masses With Children* are specifically devoted to readings and presentation of them in a Mass with children. We are encouraged to suit the readings to each group of youngsters we work with. Quality is emphasized rather than quantity. It is the responsibility of the teacher or coordinator to make the readings comprehensible to the group. The Gospel is the good news. We want to help the children to "hear" Jesus speaking to them through the readings.

With younger children, shorten the readings. Use simple costumes and props to act them out during a Mass. Make a film of the children acting out a reading ahead of time. Use the film during the Mass celebration. Write a rebus story together (see pages 61 to 64 of the Appendix examples). Use scripture for the basis of your story. Let the group decide on pictures to use in place of words in the story. Help the children to find readings that relate to their theme and that they understand.

With the group, choose readings that match the chosen theme and the maturity level of the children. Once you have decided on which readings to use in your liturgy, you need to discuss how you will present them.

You might want to have different individuals read the readings. Your group might want to act out the readings or make a film to illustrate them. Echo-pantomime is a powerful way to present the readings. The leader stands in front of the group of children presenting the reading. The leader says one line and does a gesture to illustrate the line. The children mirror back in words and actions what was done by the leader. This continues line by line for the entire reading. Whatever way you finally decide to present the readings, try to be as flexible as the suggestions might cause you to be. "Everything depends upon the spiritual advantage which the reading can offer to children" (*Directory for Masses With Children*, 1974, paragraph 44).

The first and second readings end with the words, "This is the word of the Lord." The congregation responds, "Thanks be to God." The Gospel message ends with the priest saying, "This is the Gospel of the Lord." And the congregation answers, "Praise to you, Lord Jesus Christ." Be sure to review these responses with your group. Whatever way you decide to present the readings, practice. And do practice the responses too. As the children become a part of the praying community of the parish, they need to more fully participate in the worship of God through joining in reciting the prayers and responses at the Mass. They are ready to learn if we are willing to instruct.

XVIII. Response

The response to the readings is presented between the Old Testament reading and the New Testament reading from the letters of Paul, James, Peter, John and Jude. It is our answer to God. God speaks to us through scripture and we respond. Usually this response takes the form of one of David's psalms from the *Book of Psalms* in the *Old Testament*.

To aid the children's understanding of the psalm response, review some of the psalms in the *Bible*. There are one hundred fifty psalms in the *Book of Psalms*. Some are very short and some are quite long. They cover a wide range of topics and always allude to man's relation to God. The psalms are poetic.

Many psalms have been put to music. Find some to present to your group of children. Some even have filmstrips to accompany the words. Using one of these presentations to begin this session with the youngsters will help them to identify with this part of the Mass. The Israelites would enter the temple singing the psalms and dancing. This might be an appropriate time to introduce gestures and other dance forms to your liturgical planning. *A Dancing People* and *Actions, Gestures & Bodily Attitudes* are good resources. *Simple Gifts*, volume 1, also has lots of practical suggestions readily adaptable to planning sessions that incorporate dance and gestures.

Ask the children to write down some of their own ideas or share with the group verbally. Tape record the session. The boys and girls should be expressing thoughts on the theme. Read the chosen readings and ask them to pick out words that particularly strike them as related to the theme. Let them share what they feel God is saying to them through the stories in scripture.

After you have collected their ideas, put them together in some type of orderly fashion. Make it as poetic as possible. Ask a parent or group of parents to help you. Use the "new" psalm at Mass.

Talk to the group about accompaniment. Would they like music and slides? Would they like a dance or gestures? What musical talents among the group can be used to enhance the presentation of the response? Perhaps the children like a particular filmstrip and song that is professionally produced. Use what best fits your theme and what speaks best to the children. This is their opportunity to speak to God after He has called to them.

XIX. Homily

On the Sabbath day, when Jesus went to the synagogue, he was often given a scroll of the Prophet Isaiah to read. Immediately afterwards, he would speak to the assembly. Thus, the synagogue service took the form of a reading followed by a commentary. Our Mass does the same. The homily is a talk on the word of God. It usually makes scripture apply to today's problems. The homily is meant to have the word of God emerge as an invitation and a summons to do God's will.

Furthermore, it has the responsibility of making clear the present relevance of the word of God. To do this, the homilist must first explain the meaning of the message. When speaking to children, this is best done by using simple, direct language. The *Directory for Masses With Children* (Paragraph 24) says:

"With the consent of the pastor or rector of the church, one of the adults may speak to the children after the gospel, especially if the priest finds it difficult to adapt himself to the mentality of the children."

Preaching to children is not easy. Sometimes the children can help find someone. One student volunteered his dad to speak on the topic of family. He felt his dad would have lots to share, and he did!

There are many ways to present the homily. One method is to incorporate the decorations into the homily. Using the theme of family, one group of children decided to make animal families for banners. As work progressed on the banners, everyone began talking about Shawn's camel family or Rochelle's bird family. The animals began to have identities of their own. The group invited the pastor to talk about their banners during his homily for their family Mass. The children reasoned that by pointing out the banners to the school community, everyone would remember that animal families need our love and protection and respect just as much as human families. This example shows how simple banner making can become a preaching tool.

Another technique is to develop a flannel board story on the theme. A little boy named Tommy has a problem with his flower collection. The flowers are compared to the apostles who, in Luke's gospel, are arguing about who is the "greatest" (Luke 9:46-48). This problem fits the theme of family, for who has not experienced the feelings of "I'm better than you" in family squabbles? This story shows that Jesus is well aware of our problems because he had friends who acted much the same way as our brothers and sisters sometimes do.

Here is the story:

Tommy loved flowers. His mom and dad helped him make a collection of pressed flowers. One night Tommy had a dream. The flowers in his collection were arguing about which was the best. The poppy said, "I'm the best. I'm golden like the sun."

The zinnia said, "I'm the best. I have hundreds of petals."

The snapdragon said, "I'm best! I can hold a little boy's hand."

The petunia cried, "I'm the best. I have millions of brothers and sisters."

"I'm white and pure," yelled a lily. "Surely you will agree there's no better flower than me!"

"Everyone knows daffodils are superb," said the daffodil with a perky grin. Then the tulip and rose started shouting. Poor Tommy. He did not know what to do. He decided to invite his friends from school to a party. At his party he told everyone to pick a flower. Bob wanted the zinnia. Helen picked the poppy. Johnny chose the snapdragon. Frank liked the petunia. Celia prefered the lily. Eileen chose the daffodil. Ross grabbed the rose, and Audrey claimed the tulip. No two friends chose the same flower. Then Tommy pinned the flowers to their new owners. *Everyone* was happy.

Simple characters can be made to illustrate the story on a flannel board. Or characters can be attached to sticks and held up as the storyteller draws out the tale.

The flannel board story is a good lead into a dialogue homily. Key questions will focus the youngster's attention on the various facets of the story that relate to the scripture reading shared earlier. Ask: What is the connection between Jesus' friends and the flowers? Who is the greatest? This is a very real question. Sometimes we say it differently. Members of a family say, "Who is best? Who is loved more? Who is spoiled? Who gets away with everything?" All these point to the original question, Who is the greatest?

St. Luke tells us the apostles were arguing. Sometimes we argue. We call each other names. Does name calling make us feel better? Did the arguing of the flowers answer the question about greatness? Jesus, like Tommy, has some good answers for us, if we will listen. St. Matthew tells us to be like little children. What did Tommy's friends do? Were they worried about which flower was the greatest? No, they were free from worry. They were happy to be treated. Have you ever been treated? Do you remember the feeling you experienced at the time? Jesus has treated us to His father's love. We are all God's children.

Tommy answered the flowers' question. What did he do? The flowers became "gifts" to others. They were shared and in the sharing came peace and happiness. How do you feel when someone shares with you? One of the most important things to remember in our story is to know that it does not matter who is the greatest. What does matter is that we know that we are chosen by God, and each of us is a special gift to someone else. If we know these two things we will also know that we can all be hapy with God forever.

One final suggestion to the homilist is to use an object lesson for the homily. Object lessons take simple articles and use them to make the message more tangible. There are many resources available that provide a wide variety of presentations. *Little Threads* is excellent. *61 Worship Talks for Children* and *To the Kid in the Pew: 60 Chapel Talks* are also good. *Kirigami* and *Origami for Christians* are more difficult, but provide variety.

The homily is an opportunity to relate the life of Jesus to the lives of the children in your group. It is not a time to take advantage of a captive audience. The best advice is to encourage the homilist to be concise and as tangible as possible. One message is better than twenty. Give the youngsters something they can remember. Do not overwhelm them with too much material.

XX. Creed

Directly after the homily, comes the Creed. The Creed is an integral part of the liturgy. It is our profession of faith, our proclamation that we believe in one Lord, one faith, and one baptism. How do we lead children to full participation of this part of the Mass? The *Directory for Masses With Children* offers the option of using the Apostles' Creed in place of the Nicene Creed. But for some children, especially younger children, the meaningful expression of their faith in their own words aids their understanding.

One group of children answered the question, What do you believe about your family? The theme for their celebration was family. Their responses included: I believe the people in my family love each other; I believe our families care about one another; I believe that my family helps me when I am in trouble. The children gained a certain increase of pride in the family unit after this litany of beliefs.

By expressing their beliefs about the theme, the children are able to understand more fully the meaning of the prayers expressing belief in God. The Creed is not just another prayer. It has a very specific purpose in the Mass. It tells everyone what we believe about our God.

At another celebration for family, family members were asked to write down and share what they believed about their own family experience. One family was chosen to share their beliefs at the Mass. The father wrote:

"First and foremost, I believe my family is special. Probably most people would make that kind of statement, but I firmly believe my family is special in that Our Lord has manifested Himself in so many ways to my family. Beginning with what my mother has told me about her parents and especially her grandfather, the circumstances which brought us together to formulate our immediate family, particularly in the last eight years, makes me believe that my family is extra special in God's eyes. Consequently, because of our family experiences we have each attained a greater awareness and realization of God which other families may not have had with regular, more "normal" experiences. While experiences in my family have been far from easy, the love, trust and care that I feel for my family makes it impossible to want it any other way."

The mother noted:

"What I believe about my family — first — is what they believe about me! The confidence and faith my own parents showed in me encouraged (not made) me want to do my best and stick with my values and beliefs. A family is a support group — like an Indian tipi — all members are independently set in their own spot, but lean together and meet at a common point. Like the tipi, however, there is a necessary "breathing space," a hole through which smoke can escape for the *life* of the family occurs inside the circle of supports, not outside. My family for me immediately is my husband. What I believe in is his faith, his unwavering values, his conviction that our family is meant to be a firm building stone. I believe, I know, our family is rooted in Christ. The very fact that we have arrived "on the side" of the death of a two year old son, cancer in our oldest son and the suicide of a parent is a blazing message that our family is important as a family! It would be logical to be bitter, and inward, but we are not. It is the Lord working in our tipi. I believe creating and maintaining a family is a full-time, life-long commitment."

The oldest son recorded:

"I believe my family is very special. I love my family and they love me. I think that we stand very well in our community. We have loving neighbors and good friends. God blesses my family very often with gifts of the Spirit. I love my family very much."

The second son jotted down:

"I believe my family looks upon me as a boy who likes to try things. I like to do anything new (Within reason!). I believe my family loves each other. My family goes to Mass every Sunday. So, I believe my family is very religious. My family is very believable!"

Listening to this particular family's beliefs during Mass was very moving. The family was too shy to read their own thoughts. The celebrant did it for them. None of the impact was lost for all who heard had tears in their eyes. We knew the family and their struggles had touched us.

The Creed is an opportunity for members of the community to share the treasures of their hearts. It has that quality of being able to draw us closer as a praying community. In sharing our beliefs, we do share one Lord, one faith and one baptism. (See Appendix pages 65-67 for more samples.

XXI. Prayers of the Faithful

The Liturgy of the Word concludes with the Prayers of the Faithful or Presidential Prayers. Why do we pray? We pray because we believe God is in our midst. We believe He will hear us and answer us. The Prayers of the Faithful follow a basic format. First there is petition. Next there is a call to prayer which is quickly followed by a communal response. Some sample petitions include: For our moms and dads, for peace in the world, for an end to the threat of nuclear war. The call to prayer is generally "We pray to the Lord." The communal response, like the petitions, varies.

Some forms of communal responses include: Lord hear our prayer; Lord hear us and answer; Lord, have mercy. These may be said or sung by the congregation. Your group might decide to act out, pantomime or film the petitions. You might choose to use sign language for the response. This can be very powerful and truly focus attention on the petitions.

During the planning session with the children, try to encourage the group to relate their prayers to their own life experience. The prayers should also reflect the theme you have chosen. Begin with a prayer experience. Then brainstorm ideas for petitions. As a group, compose five or six petitions. Choose an appropriate response or make up one. Finally, decide on the method you will use for presentation of the petitions during the celebration of the Mass. Will children volunteers read single petitions? Will you make a film? Will you use slides? What about dance?

The Prayers of the Faithful end with a prayer. See the section on Prayers in an earlier section of this chapter. The Prayers of the Faithful marks the end of the Liturgy of the Word. It reflects the children's insight into the readings. It also shows how they hope to apply the readings to their daily living.

XXII. Offertory

The Liturgy of the Eucharist begins with the Preparation of the Gifts. (See Appendix page 68.) What is a party without gifts? During the Mass, gifts are offered. Begin this session with your group by telling a story or presenting an object lesson that focuses on gift-giving.

Talk about the traditional gifts of wine and bread. Wine and bread are both symbols of unity. Wine comes from many grapes. Bread comes from many grains of wheat. Both the grapes and the grains are crushed to make one cup of wine and one loaf of bread. At Mass, many gather to make one Church.

Include bread and wine in the list of gifts to be offered at Mass. Discuss with your group of children the theme you have chosen for the Mass. Let the theme generate ideas from the youngsters for other gifts that might be offered. Brainstorm ideas together.

In planning a Mass celebrating the family, one group of primary-aged children suggested job flowers. Each child made a flower with jobs written on the petals. During Mass, the flowers were presented to the parents, who were to give the child a petal when a job needed to be done. Another suggestion was candles, which represent Jesus, the Light of the World. The children brought up candles to the altar, then gave their parents a candle for home. The families used their candles on their dinner table; they lit them before each meal and prayed together.

Accept all suggestions during the brainstorming session. Afterward, eliminate impractical ideas. Materials available and time will be major considerations when you are thinking about the possibilities. Pick only two or three gifts in addition to the bread and wine. Write a short explanation of each gift for the Mass booklet, such as the following:

We bring a Bible to show the love we have for God.
We bring food as a sign that we want to help the poor.
We bring a cross because Jesus died for our sins.

Take some time to consider how your group will present their gifts during the Mass. You might choose to explain the gifts before they are brought to the altar. Or the gifts might be carried up to the altar while the congregation sings an appropriate song. After the song, a reader might explain each gift as the presentor holds or elevates the gift for all to see. Talk to your celebrant and be sure to consider the structure of the Church setting. Do not forget to get volunteers to carry the gifts up to the altar.

XXIII. Eucharistic Prayer

The Eucharistic Prayer is "the center and highpoint of the entire celebration," "a prayer of thanksgiving and sanctification" in which "the whole congregation joins Christ in acknowledging the works of God and in offering the sacrifice." This definition from the *General Instruction of the Roman Missal* (no. 54) applies both to adults and to children. The Eucharistic Prayer makes up the second portion of the Liturgy of the Eucharist. Everything should be done to make the children as attentive as possible to this part of the Mass.

Use an object lesson or prayer experience to begin this session with the youngsters. Tell the story of the Last Supper. Find a filmstrip that describes the Last Supper and share it with your group. Ask some boys and girls to pantomime or act out the story as you read it from scripture.

The Eucharistic Prayer is primarily a prayer of praise and thanksgiving. It has several other elements. It gives an overview of salvation history; it asks God to send the Spirit to bless our gifts; it retells the story of the Last Supper; it reminds us of Jesus, His passion, death and resurrection; it summarizes our faith; and it petitions the Father for concerns around the world. The Prayer ends with the words, "Through Him, with Him, in Him, in the unity of the Holy Spirit, all glory and honor is yours almighty Father, for ever and ever."

Several Eucharistic Prayers have been approved for use at children's Masses. One puts emphasis on the Santus. The second incorporates responses throughout the prayer. The third includes responses and also options for the Easter season. Prior to your celebration, read them through. Choose the one that best accomodates your theme and meets the needs of your group. Be sure to go over the Prayer with your group prior to celebration of the Mass.

With the children, decide how to present the Sanctus, Proclamation of Faith and Great Amen. Will you sing them or say them? If you choose a Eucharistic Prayer with other responses, will you sing them or say them? The final part of the Liturgy of the Eucharist is the Communion Rite. It includes the Lord's Prayer. Choose a method of presentation for this prayer also.

XXIV. Sign of Peace

At this time in the Mass, we reach out to "touch" the hearts of our neighbors. Jesus said to love your neighbor as you love yourself. We show this love by some sign, by giving this sign to our neighbor. Peace signs include: drawings, hearts, holy cards of saints, special homemade cards, dried flowers, poems, pretzels (during Lent), and signing (in sign language).

Use an energizer to introduce this planning session. Tell your youngsters that the best way to understand an energizer and how it works is to participate. Ask everyone to make a choice. Choose to be a giver, a receiver or a watcher. Wait a few moments and say, "Hopefully each of you has picked one! If you are a giver, please stand. Giving is an important part of family and of friendship. Givers have a sign. Shake hands with someone close to you." Give participants time to follow the instructions. Then ask them to remain standing.

Next, ask the receivers to stand. Say, "Receivers too have a sign. When someone does something nice for us, we smile and say 'Thank you'". Allow time for instructions to be followed. Then ask the receivers to remain standing.

Only one group should still be seated. Ask the watchers to stand. Everyone in the room should be standing. Say, "We always expect positive feedback from watchers, especially in our family situations. Watchers, your sign is a gentle pat on the back. Turn to someone close and give them a gentle pat on the back." Pause and allow time for the task to be completed.

Say to the entire group, "I hope everyone has been paying attention. Through life, we are sometimes givers, receivers and watchers. Our roles change with situations and circumstances. Now we proceed to the big test. Remember our key words to our signs. If I say 'givers,' we shake hands. If I say 'receivers,' we smile and say 'Thank you.' If I say 'watchers,' give a gentle pat on the back to someone close. Ready? Let us all be givers. Did you remember to shake a hand? Let us all be receivers. Did you remember to smile and say, 'Thank you?' Let us all be watchers.

Did you give someone a gentle pat on the back? Be receivers, givers, watchers, givers, receivers..."

This energizer focuses on something very important. Not all children have experienced a togetherness within a group structure. Working on the Mass and its planning sessions enables your group to energize itself and provides an important community sharing for the children. This feeling of togetherness and fun permeates the planning sessions and is fulfilled in the Mass celebration itself. It is during the Rite of Peace that the energy made evident in the planning sessions will find expression by our reaching out and greeting one another and meaning it with the words of Christ Himself, "Peace be with you."

After the energizer, tell the children that during the Mass there is a time when Christian energy is given one to another. It is a time when we show that we all are friends. Brainstorm expressions of friendship. Ask what friends do when they say hel-lo. Friends shake hands, kiss, hug and exchange gifts. You might want to do some role playing.

Children have a wealth of ideas. One child suggested passing out crosses made from twigs for an Ash Wednesday Mass. Another young girl wanted to teach sign language to the congregation. She said to say only three words in sign, Christ's peace be with you. In planning a special Mass for forgiveness, one child suggested choosing about ten youngsters to carry small candles up the aisle to the altar. The youngsters were to stop on the altar and form a cross. We darkened the Church for the Sign of Peace. The children processed up the main aisle while the organist played "Let There Be Peace On Earth."

First Communicants wanted their parents to make the sign of the cross on their foreheads. Then they wanted to give the sign of peace to members of their own families. Third graders planned a special Mass for peace in Ireland. For the sign of peace, they carried cards up the main aisle of the Church while the organist played "Make Me a Channel of Your Peace." The cards spelled out the letters for the words, Peace in Ireland! Then the group processed over to a side wall of the Church and taped up the message. They incorporated the Sign of Peace in their decorations for the Church.

Whatever you choose for the Sign of Peace, be sure to explain it briefly prior to presentation during the Mass. Include a brief explanation in the Mass booklet. Options for this part of the Mass help the children to focus on its importance. Jesus reached out to people and touched them to heal them. We need to help our children to find appropriate ways to reach out to one another during our celebrations.

XXV. *Communion*

After the Sign of Peace, the priest breaks the bread. In sharing the one bread, we show our unity in faith. The celebrant prays silently, then calls us to communion with our Lord. He says, "Behold the Lamb of God who takes away the sins of the world. Happy are we who are called to his supper." The community responds, "Lord, I am not worthy to receive you, but only say the word and I shall be healed."

Communion is given to all by the priest and Ministers of the Eucharist. Ask your group if their parents, brothers, sisters, or friends are Ministers of the Eucharist. Before inviting them to participate, be sure to discuss this with the celebrant.

The Liturgy of the Eucharist concludes with a prayer asking God to help us integrate all we have shared at the Mass into our daily lives. See the previous section on Prayer for guidelines for planning this.

XXVI. Blessing

The Closing Rite is composed of two parts, the Blessing and the Dismissal (see Appendix page 69). To introduce the planning session for the Blessing, tell the story of Jacob and Essau (Genesis 27). A blessing is a special gift. It is hope for the future expressed in a prayer form. It is asking God to extend some gift to those we love and care about.

The *Directory for Masses With Children* encourages the use of richer forms of blessing in children's liturgies. Additional blessings can be found in the *Sacramentary*, but most are beyond the understanding of primary-aged children. Talk to your group about your theme. What gifts do they wish for those who will be attending the celebration of the Mass they are planning? Brainstorm ideas.

You can use this planning session as an opportunity to develop the group's appreciation for the three Persons in one God. Talk about God the Father. What qualities stand out in the children's minds about God the Father. Is He creator? Is He almighty? Is He all-powerful? What gift would they like from the Father for themselves and those they love? First graders wrote, "May God, our loving Father, bless you with His goodness and love so you learn to be good." Third graders prayed, "May God, maker of the world, bless you with His forgiveness."

Talk about Jesus, the Son of God. How would the group describe Jesus? Is He savior? Is He brother? What gift would they like from Jesus for themselves and those who attend their Mass? Kindergarteners said, "May Jesus, our brother, give you peace in your life." Second graders prayed, "May Jesus, the loving Son of God, bless you and keep you from committing sins."

A discussion about the Holy Spirit will aid the boys' and girls' knowledge of the Third Person of the Blessed Trinity. Help the children to develop some descriptive phrases for the Holy Spirit. When he ascended into Heaven, Jesus sent the Holy Spirit to the apostles. Second graders prayed, "May the Holy Spirit, the Spirit of Light, help you to get a better education in school and help you to work for better grades." First graders wrote, "May the Holy Spirit bless you with life and help you to be kind to one another."

Another option for the blessing is to choose a song and share the blessing by singing. "Sabbath Prayer" is a good choice for this part of the

Mass. Be open to the suggestions of the group. And be sure to discuss ideas with the celebrant. The priest might introduce the children's blessing by recalling special moments in the Mass, reminding the children of their commitments to God. He would conclude with the final blessing, retaining the trinitarian formula with the sign of the cross at the end.

XXVII. Dismissal

The end of Mass is a new beginning for each Christian who participates. We are "sent" forth on a mission. We are told by the priest to "go." This is a strong message. We are told to go "in peace." Explore with your group their feelings about peace and harmony. What does it mean to be a Christian?

In the planning session for songs, you can guide the children to pick an ending song that is strong. You might think of one that the group can march to. The boys and girls might also have ideas about some Christian action they can now become involved in to carry out the message of their prayers at Mass.

Do not forget to plan some follow-up activities for the planners. The Mass is not an isolated event to be forgotten as soon as it is over. It is an ongoing celebration of where we are at a particular moment in time. Make it an integral part of your group's praying experiences.

XXVIII. Closing Remarks

These suggestions for Mass planning are made to enhance the participation of the children and to help their understanding of what is being celebrated. It is important to remember that the Eucharist is a celebration of the Lord who is among us. You know your children best. Your efforts to draw out the particular talents or gifts of those children will certainly be richly rewarded.

Pope John Paul II said to the youth when he was in the United States, "You and I and all of us together make up the Church...Only in Christ do we find real love and the fullness of life. So I invite you today to look to Christ." What closer look can we give to our children than to offer them full participation in our Eucharistic celebrations.

Your Masses will not be perfect. There will be mistakes. You are working with children. You have done all you can by the time you get to the Church or place designated for your celebration. If you are nervous, the children will be more so. The best advice is "Let go!" Receive the gift of your children's talents. They will certainly, if you have freed them to celebrate in their own way, shout the Gospel with their lives.

I hope that this liturgy book will provide you with a useful tool to add to your liturgical resources for planning prayer experiences with youngsters. It is an attempt to facilitate an already existing process. Catholic educators are now strongly encouraged to provide youngsters with prayer expressions that enhance their faith life. And they are seeking resources to assist them. Chapter IV is a review of other work on the topic of children's liturgy.

Conclusion

How to Plan Children's Liturgies appears to be a helpful aid to teachers. Feedback from participants in workshops and co-workers so far validates this. Comments on workshop evaluation forms included: "Good," "Excellent! Almost too much crammed in," "Very well planned! Instructors showed a lot of enthusiasm and information." On the whole, participants of workshops approved of the lessons. Co-workers have requested copies of the manuscripts.

The method presented helps teachers to be more independent. Teachers are freed from the worry of developing their own method or technique for planning liturgies. They are provided with a workable method that is easy to follow. Most educators in the Catholic schools and in catechetical programs are required to plan prayer experiences with their group. Many fumble through the experience. Like myself, some have devised a system of their own through the process of trial and error. Others rely on prepackaged liturgies adapting them to meet the needs of their own group of children. *How to Plan Children's Liturgies* does not plan for the teacher. It shows the teacher or instructor how to plan with the children.

How to Plan Children's Liturgies instructs the Catholic educator in approved structures of the Mass for children. The work is based on information promulgated by the Catholic Church in the document, *The Directory for Masses With Children*. I am familiar with Edward Matthews' commentary on the Directory. Edward Matthews was part of the team that wrote the Directory. And his commentary draws out for the reader the full meaning and intent of the document. *How to Plan Children's Liturgies* closely follows those guides.

Using the method recommended in *How to Plan Children's Liturgies*, Chapter II of this work helps to support and develop community among the instructor and participants. Children are asked to share their ideas and talents. Instructors are directed to listen and to utilize the gifts and talents of their students. Experiences are shared. The group prays and plays together. In sharing our ideas, we share a bit of our own story, a bit of who we are as people. This is the basis for community. We come together and share who we are with one another. Planning an activity together is a community building project in itself.

Just as the educator learns a technique following the guides throughout Chapter II, the children also learn a way of doing something. They learn how a Mass develops. They learn that it is a community project. It is not the result of one person's thoughts, but rather the expression of many people's thoughts. They learn to appreciate the Mass as part of their own lives. It becomes important to them when they participate in its planning and execution. One student shared, "The Mass was extra-special and was very creative." Another wrote, "Even when I'm older I will still remember all of the Masses we've planned..."

The children benefit in a positive way when their own work is used and appreciated. Their self-worth and self-concept are enhanced because their ideas are affirmed. They not only see their work, but also look for it. Children read the Mass guide if their pictures are used to illustrate it. They encourage their parents to attend their Masses when they have been involved in the planning and sharing of the mass celebration.

Recommendations

After use of the method in one school for two years, I would also suggest that educators within a single learning environment agree on and adopt one method for use within that environment for planning liturgies. The students of Our Lady of the Rosary School in Union City, California, began to appreciate the Mass to a greater degree after use of the suggested method throughout the school for two years. They learned the process the first year and were more adept at its implementation the second year. A sense of community developed throughout the school focused on the monthly Mass celebration. Students as well as teachers expressed a comfortableness with the Mass neither group had experienced before.

Planning children's liturgies is not an impossible task. It is a good experience when children are involved. They bring life to the activity. They renew the spirit of joy that all ages need to experience. I encourage all readers to involve children in their Mass planning. They certainly are your greatest resource!

Review of Related Literature

Anyone working in the field of liturgy must first be cognizant of the Church's documents specifically relating to liturgy. It is important to consider the contents of these documents in any study of the Mass as they form the framework for the approved structure of the Mass. *The Liturgy Documents* published by Liturgy Training Program provides a collection of seven documents: "The Constitution on the Sacred Liturgy," "The 1967 Instruction on Eucharistic Worship," "The General Instruction on the New Roman Missal with the Appendix for the United States," "General Norms for the Liturgical Year," "Directory for Masses with Children," "Music in Catholic Worship," and "Environment and Art in Catholic Worship." "This present resource book is intended to provide parish personnel with a handy copy of seven of the most basic post-Vatican II documents on liturgy" (Huck, 1980, p.ii).

Other Church documents on this topic, important for consideration, include: *Sharing the Light of Faith, Synod of Bishops — 1977, To Teach As Jesus Did,* and *Catechist* by Pope John Paul II. These documents are addressed to parents and teachers in their role as catechist. They provide important guidelines for education in Catholicism. A good liturgist will be familiar with them in addition to the documents specifically relating to liturgy.

To understand the basic components of the Mass, a review of the historical development of this prayer form is pertinent. Several works explain the Mass: *The Once and Future Liturgy* by J. D. Crichton, Diekman's *Come, Let Us Worship, The Mass Explained,* by Rev. Thomas McMahon, and two pamphlets, *The Mass: Everybody's Celebration* by Joanne McPortland and *The Roots of the Mass* both published by St. Francis Productions. Most of these works give historical background on the structure of the Mass. They tell how different rituals developed and what changes have occurred. J. D. Cichton even considers what the future Mass will be like. All are good resources for understanding the various parts of the Mass and the whys and wherefores for placement and changes.

In our review of literature, we also need to consider the child. "How to Plan Children's Liturgies," the title of this book, focuses not only on liturgy, but also on children. How is faith developed? How can faith be communicated to children? *A Learning Process for Religious Education,*

Bringing Up Children in the Christian Faith, Children and Adolescents, Exploring the Bible with Children, Will Our Children Have Faith, and *Sharing our Biblical Story* all consider the religious formation of youth. They provide the religious educator with some facts about children and how they learn. Very young children need concrete experiences, indeed, these are the essence of childhood.

"To have Christian faith, each of us needs to retain or recapture the imagination and wonder of our childhood. We need to experience again the spontaneity, creativity, and excitement we knew as children. We need to live with a sense of dependent openness; to explore, look, hear, taste, and smell; to experience a sense of awe; to enjoy holy leisure and festivity" (Westerhoff, 1980, p. 19). Westerhoff (1980) goes on to say that "children live in a world of the senses" (p. 20). As catechists we need to recognize this and utilize learning experiences that capitalize on it.

Michael Warren (1977) adequately poses a vital question in his article titled, "Can the Liturgy Speak to Today's Teenagers?" He says, "Only when the Sunday eucharist (or daily eucharist) is fitting into a context of prayer in my total life do I find that my own personal participation in eucharistic liturgy has the quality of response it should have" (p. 16). Does the liturgy we plan for children fit into their lives? Are we providing experiences of prayer at Masses for children that invite them to actively participate?

Most liturgy resource books available for use with youth provide "packaged" liturgy services. The services are planned already. The liturgist need only follow the prayer given in the book. Some of these resources include: *The Blessing Cup, Celebrate Wonder, Children's Liturgies, Everything You Need for Children's Worship (Except Children), The Experimental Liturgy Book, Family Worship Idea Book, Holy Days & Holidays, How Green Is Green, Liturgies for Children, Liturgies for Little Ones, On Cloud Nine, Run With Him,* and *Touching God.* These are all sample liturgy books. Everything needed is provided. The only exception, as indicated by one of the titles, is the children themselves. For someone inexperienced in the field of chidren's liturgy, these resources provide a starting point. They show how a liturgy is done. They do not provide the spontaneity of children.

Other resources enhance participation of the various parts of the Mass. *Experiments in Growth* and *Experiments in Prayer* develop techniques for prayer. *Child's Play, The Bible as Drama, How the Word Became Flesh, Lectionary for Children's Mass, Liturgy of the Word for Children,* and *This is the Word of the Lord* offer ideas for developing the readings in the Mass. *Bible Object Talks with Paper and Scissors, Good News from Matthew, The Gospel for Children, Kirigami, Little Threads, The Irritated Oyster & Other Object Lessons for Children, The Droopy Flower Mystery and Other Object Lessons for Children, Origami for Christians, Preaching the New Lectionary, 61 Worship Talks for Children* and *To the Kid in the Pew: 60 Chapel Talks* give ideas for development of the homily. *Bread Blessed and Broken* describes the eucharistic prayer. *Liturgical Celebration: Possible Patterns* gives some detail regarding the components of the eucharistic prayer. And *Eucharistic Prayers for Children* contains three eucharistic prayers for children's Masses that have been approved by the Holy See.

Several works contain suggestions for more than one part of the Mass. Some offer one basic idea that can be applied to the different parts of the Mass. *The Joy of Signing* teaches sign language. It could be used for the sign of peace, response for the prayers of the faithful or part of the communion meditation. *A Dancing People* teaches the art of dance. Any of the various responses in the Mass might be expressed through dance. *Actions, Gestures & Bodily Attitudes* shows use of the whole body in many parts of the Mass.

Simple Gifts has two volumes. Both are compilations of liturgy articles published in *Liturgy* magazine. They contain lots of practical suggestions easily adaptable to children's liturgies and the planning of those liturgies. *The Lord Blesses Me* is a good resource for those working with children. It provides centering activities that focus on the greeting, the Word of God, sharing and witnessing. One final work that also falls into this category is *Mime: The Technique of Silence*. This work develops an appreciation for silence that is very important in the prayer life of children.

"Even in Masses with children 'silence should be observed at the proper times as a part of the celebration' lest too great a role be given to external action. In their own way children are genuinely capable of reflection. They need, however, a kind of introduction so that they will learn how to reflect within themselves, meditate briefly, or praise God and pray to him in their hearts for example after the homily or after communion" (*Directory for Masses with Children*, 1973, Paragraph 37). All of these works provide stimuli for the planner. They offer creative suggestions for revitalizing aspects of liturgy. They are not prepackaged. They are not in a final form. They leave to the reader some degree of decision as to their usage.

One other liturgy book takes a step back from prepackaging liturgy. *The Welcome Table* includes the document, *Directory for Masses with Children*. It also gives background and suggestions for enhancing various aspects of the Mass. It provides thoughtful reflection on the purpose of parts of the Mass. It is an excellent resource for those working with children planning liturgical celebrations.

No books or articles that provide lesson plans are available to teachers who would like to plan Masses or liturgies with children. There are no studies which indicate the validity of existing literature. Certainly this review is not exhaustive of all work on the topic of children's liturgy. It does, however, cover much of what is available at this time. It is an indication that there is much that can be done in this field of study.

In summary, the *Directory for Masses with Children* is the key Catholic Church document relating liturgical worship to the life of the child. Other documents outline worship for adults. Literature is available describing the roots of the Mass and the spiritual development of the child. Children's liturgy books generally can be divided into three categories. First, there are books of the prepackaged liturgy variety. A Mass is planned for every season and type of celebration. Next, there are books that develop one aspect of the Mass. These are excellent resources for ideas for developing parts of the Mass with different groups. The third category is made up of books like *The Welcome Table*. These books are not quite lesson plans. Yet they are not prepackaged liturgies either. They are resource books for the catechist. They empower the catechist to understand the motivation behind the structure of the various parts of the Mass. They motivate innovation.

How to Plan Children's Liturgies would be in a fourth category. The typical catechist does not have the time to develop teaching techniques for the various subjects that must be covered in any religion course. How to Plan Children's Liturgies provides step by step directives for planning liturgical celebrations with primary-aged children. It does not plan them for the teacher. It does not give ideas for the various parts of the Mass. It does encourage the teacher to stimulate the children in his/her group to share their own ideas.

After reviewing related literature, one can see a progression since the publication of the *Directory for Masses with Children*. It would seem that authors first shared their own ideas and successes. These are the prepackaged liturgies. Then, they began to focus on one aspect of liturgy or one technique such as dance. This was a step from the general to the specific. *The Welcome Table* is more of a reflective nature. We stop to consider what the purpose of each part of the Mass was originally. I believe that *How to Plan Children's Liturgies* is the next step in the progression. If we accept that liturgy is "expressive action," then we must attempt to find a way for children to speak to God using their own language. Chapter II is an attempt to give you the tools to facilitate this expression.

Bibliography

Abbot, W.M., ed. *The Documents of Vatican II*. New York: Guild Press, 1966.

Aurelio, J. *Story Sunday*. New York: Paulist Press, 1978.

Bell, M. *The Way of the Wolf*. New York: The Seabury Press, 1961.

Brown, F.C. *Bible Object Talks with Paper and Scissors*. Cincinnati: Standard Publishing, 1976.

Brandt, L.F. *God Is Here — Let's Celebrate*. St. Louis: Concordia Publishing, 1974.

Bucher, J.M. *Run with Him*. Cincinnati: North American Liturgy Resources, 1974.

Caprio, B. *Experiments in Prayer*. Notre Dame: Ave Maria Press, 1974.

Caprio, B. *Experiments in Growth*. Notre Dame: Ave Maria Press, 1976.

Chilson, R. *The Way to Christianity*. Minneapolis: Winston Press, Inc., 1979.

Cronin, G.B. *Holy Days & Holidays*. Minneapolis: Winston Press, Inc., 1979.

Dallen, J. *Liturgical Celebration: Possible Patterns*. Cincinnati: North American Liturgy Resources, 1971.

Danielou, J. *The Bible and the Liturgy*. Notre Dame: University of Notre Dame Press, 1956.

Deitering, C. *Actions, Gestures & Bodily Attitudes*. San Jose: Resource Publications, Inc., 1980.

Diekman, G. *Come, Let Us Worship*. Garden City: Image Books, 1961.

Directory for Masses with Children. Washington Publications Office, United States Catholic Conference, 1973.

Dherty, C.D. *Not without Parables*. Notre Dame: Ave Maria Press, 1977.

Elkind, D. *Childen and Adolescents*. New York: Oxford University Press, 1981.

Faucher, W.T. *Touching God*. Notre Dame: Ave Maria Press, 1975.

Francis, D.B. *Piggy-Bank Minds and 49 Other Object Lessons for Children*. Nashville: The Parthenon Press, 1977.

Franzen, LG. *Good News from Matthew*. Minneapolis: Augsburg Publishing House, 1977.

Freburger, W.J., ed. *This Is the Word of the Lord*. Notre Dame: Ave Maria Press, 1970.

Freburger, W.J., and Haas, J.E. *Eucharistic Prayers for Children*. Notre Dame: Ave Maria Press, 1976.

Fuller, R.H. *Preaching the New Lectionary: The Word of God for the Church Today*. Collegeville: The Liturgical Press, 1971.

Furnish, D.J. *Exploring the Bible with Children*. Nashville: Abingdon Press, 1975.

Gallagher, J.V. *What Is Liturgy?* New Jersey: Paulist Press, 1962.

Gamm, D.B. *On Cloud Nine*. Notre Dame: Ave Maria Press, 1976.

Gamm, D.B. *Child's Play*. Notre Dame: Ave Maria Press, 1978.

Harmin, M,. and Sax, S. *A Peaceable Classroom: Activities to Calm and Free Student Energies*. Minneapolis: Winston Press, Inc., 1977.

Hendricks, G., and Roberts, T.B. *The Second Centering Book*, Englewood Cliffs: Prentice-Hall, Inc., 1977.

Hilliard, D. *The Lord Blesses Me*. San Jose: Resource Publications, 1978.

Hoey, R.F., ed. *The Experimental Liturgy Book*. New York: Herder and Herder, 1969.

Horda, R. *Dry Bones: Living Worship Guides to Good Liturgy*. Washington: Liturgical Conference, Inc., 1973.

Huck, G., ed. *Simple Gifts* (2 Vols.). Washington: Liturgical Conference, Inc., 1974.

Huck, G., ed. *The Liturgy Documents*. Chicago: Liturgy Training Program, 1980.

Ihli, J. *Liturgies of the Word for Children*. New York: Paulist Press, 1979.

Jamison, A. *Liturgies for Children*. Cincinnati: St. Anthony Messenger Press, 1975.

Jeep, E.M. *The Welcome Table*. Chicago: Liturgy Training Publications, 1982.

John Paul II. *Catechist*. Chicago: Franciscan Herald Press, 1980.

Joyce, B., and Showers, B. "Improving Inservice Training: The Message of Research." *Educational Leadership*, February 1980, pp. 379-385.

Kelsey, M. *The Age of Miracles*. Notre Dame: Ave Maria Press, 1979.

Kenny, B., ed. *Children's Liturgies*. New York: Paulist Press, 1977.

Kinghorn, C.J., and Landry, C. *Celebrating Jesus*. Phoenix: North American Liturgy Resources, 1977.

Kemper, F.W. *Kirigami*. St. Louis: Concordia Publishing House, 1979.

Kung, H. *On Being a Christian*. New York: Pocket Books, 1976.

Larsen, E., and Galvin, P. *Liturgy Begins at Home*. Liguori: Liguori Publications, 1973.

LeBlanc, E., and Talbot, M.R. *How Green Is Green?*. Notre Dame: Ave Maria Press, 1975.

Link, M. *The Mustard Seed*. Niles: Argus Communications, 1974.

Mahlmann, L., and Jones, D.C. *Puppet Plays from Favorite Stories*. Boston: Plays, Inc., 1977.

Marbach, E. *Once-Upon-A-Time Saints*. Cincinnati: St. Anthony Messenger Press, 1977.

Matthews, E. *Celebrating Mass with Children*. New York: Paulist Press, 1975.

May, E.C. *Family Worship Idea Book*. St. Louis: Concordia Publishing House, 1970.

Maxwell, J. *Worship in Action: A Parish Model of Creative Liturgy and Social Concern*. Mystic: Twenty-Third Publications, 1981.

McMahon, T. *The Mass Explained*. St. Paul: Carillon Books, 1977.

McPortland, J. *The Mass: Everybody's Celebration*. Los Angeles: Franciscan Communications, 1980.

McPortland, J. *The Roots of the Mass*. Los Angeles: Franciscan Communications, 1981.

Moore, H.D. *Little Threads and Other Object Lessons for Children*. Nashville: Abingdon Press, 1974.

Moore, H.D., and Moore, P.A. *The Irritated Oyster and Other Object Lessons for children*. Nashville: Abingdon Press, 1976.

Moore, H.D., and Moore, P.S. *The Droopy Flower Mystery and Other Object Lessons for Children*. Nashville: Abingdon Press, 1979.

Mossi, J.P. (Ed.). *Bread Blessed and Broken*. New York: Paulist Press, 1974.

Moynahan, M. *How the Word Became Flesh*. San Jose: Resource Publications, Inc., 1981.

Ortegel, A. *A Dancing People*. West Lafayette: The Center for Contemporary Celebration, 1976.

Peterson, J.H. *Origami for Christians*. Wilton: Morehouse-Barlow Company, Inc., 1979.

Powers, I. *Nameless Faces in the Life of Jesus*. Mystic: Twenty-Third Publications, 1981.

Reichert, R. *A Learning Process for Religious Education*. Dayton: Pflaum Press, 1975.

Ressino, A. *Celebrate Wonder*. New York: Paulist Press, 1972.

Rezy, C. *Liturgies for Little Ones*. Notre Dame: Ave Maria Press, 1978.

Riekehof, L.L. *The Joy of Signing*. Springfield: Gospel Publishing House, 1978.

Russell, J.P. *Sharing Our Biblical Story*. Minneapolis: Winston Press, Inc., 1979.

Sawyer, K. *Developing Faith*. Notre Dame: Ave Maria Press, 1978.

Schrank, J. *Teaching Human Beings*. Boston: Beacon Press, 1972.

Sharing the Light of Faith. Washington: United States Catholic Conference, 1979.

Shepard, R. *Mime the Technique of Silence*. New York: Drama Book Specialists, 1971.

Sloyan, V., and Huck, G., eds. *Children's Liturgies*. Washington: The Liturgical Conference, 1976.

Synod of Bishops — 1977. Washington: United States Catholic Conference, 1978.

Tos, A.J., ed. *Lectionary for Children's Mass*. New York: Pueblo Publishing Company, 1974.

To Teach as Jesus Did. Washington: Publications Office, United States Catholic Conference, 1973.

Travnikar, R. *The Blessing Cup*. Cincinnati: St. Anthony Messenger Press, 1970.

Uhl, H.J. *The Gospel for Children*. Minneapolis: Augsburg Publishing House, 1975.

Vincenza, M. *Creative Religion Involvement Programs*. New York: Alba House, 1973.

Waddy, L. *The Bible as Drama*. New York: Paulist Press, 1975.

Warren, M. "Can the Liturgy Speak to Today's Teenagers?" *Liturgy*, September 1977, pp. 12-18.

Weisheit, E. *Sixty-One Worship Talks for Children*. St. Louis: Concordia Publishing House, 1968.

Westerhoff, J.H. *Will Our Children Have Faith?* New York: The Seabury Press, 1976.,

Westerhoff, J.H. *Bringing up Children in the Christian Faith*. Minneapolis: Winston Press, Inc., 1980.

White, J.N. *Everything You Need for Children's Worship* *(Except Children)*. Cincinnati: St. Anthony Messenger Press, 1978.

Appendix

Essential parts of children's liturgy

    Introductory rite ...
        Explain theme
        any one element
            plus concluding prayer

    Liturgy of the Word
        Gospel

    Liturgy of the Eucharist
        Eucharistic prayer
        Lord's prayer
        breaking of the bread
        invitation to Communion

    Closing rites
        Invitation which precedes final blessing
        Blessing — some form
        Trinitarian formula
        Sign of the Cross

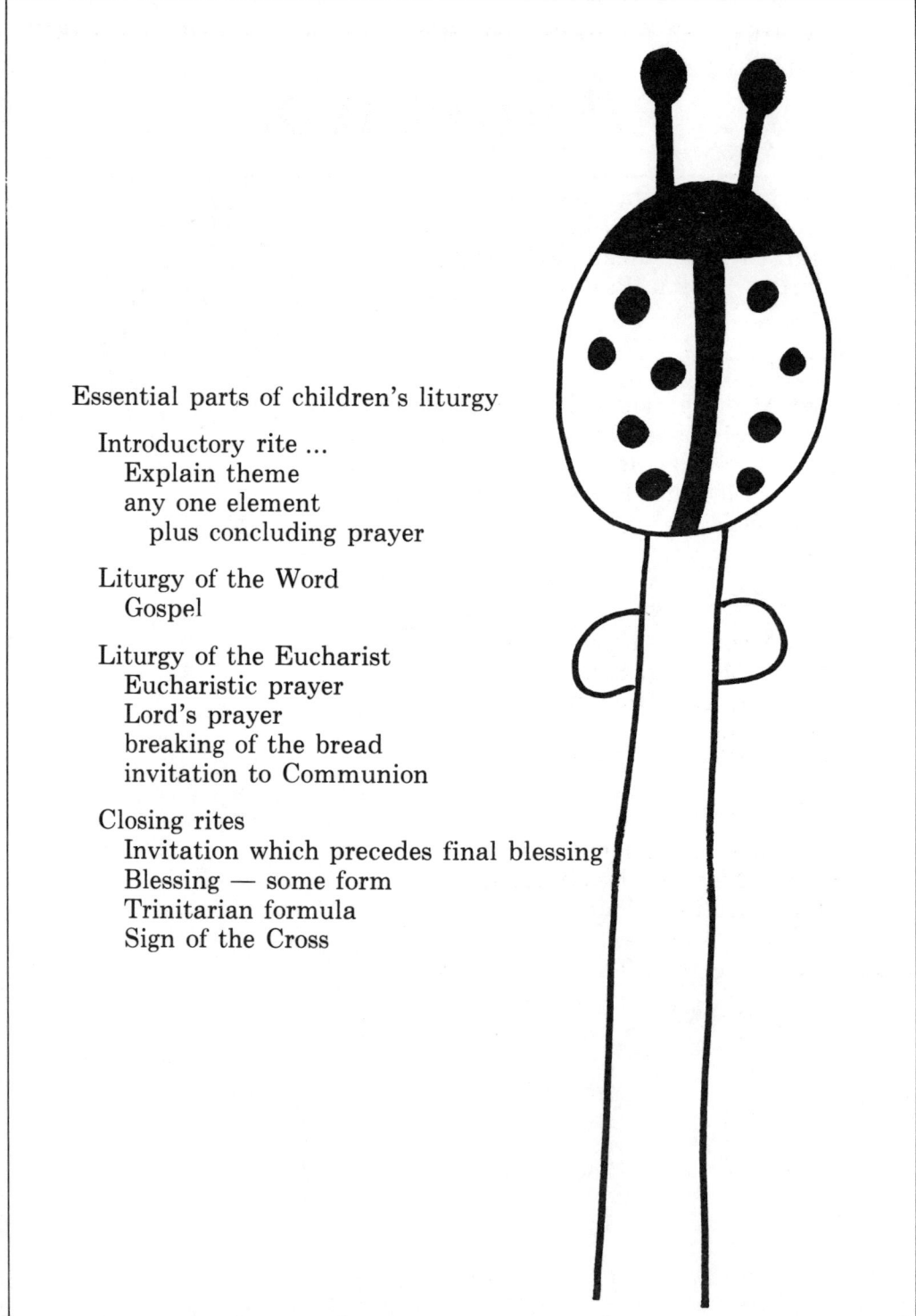

If your program meets once a week, your timeline might look like this:

First Mass

First Meeting: Mass overview and Theme
Second Meeting: Decorations, Invitations
Third Meeting: Readings, Songs
Fourth Meeting: Prayers, Blessing
Mass

Second Mass

First Meeting: Theme, Penitential Rite
Second Meeting: Decorations, Invitations
Third Meeting: Readings, Songs
Fourth Meeting: Prayers of the Faithful, Prayers
Mass

Third Mass

First Meeting: Theme, Decorations
Second Meeting: Songs, Readings
Third Meeting: Invitations, Offertory Procession
Fourth Meeting: Creed, Sign of Peace

Fourth Mass

First Meeting: Theme, Gloria
Second Meeting: Readings, Homily
Third Meeting: Eucharistic Prayer, People responses
Fourth Meeting: The Lord's Prayer
Mass

GENERAL GUIDELINES

- A. Object lesson
- B. Review
- C. Suggestions
- D. Class Assignment
- E. Group Work

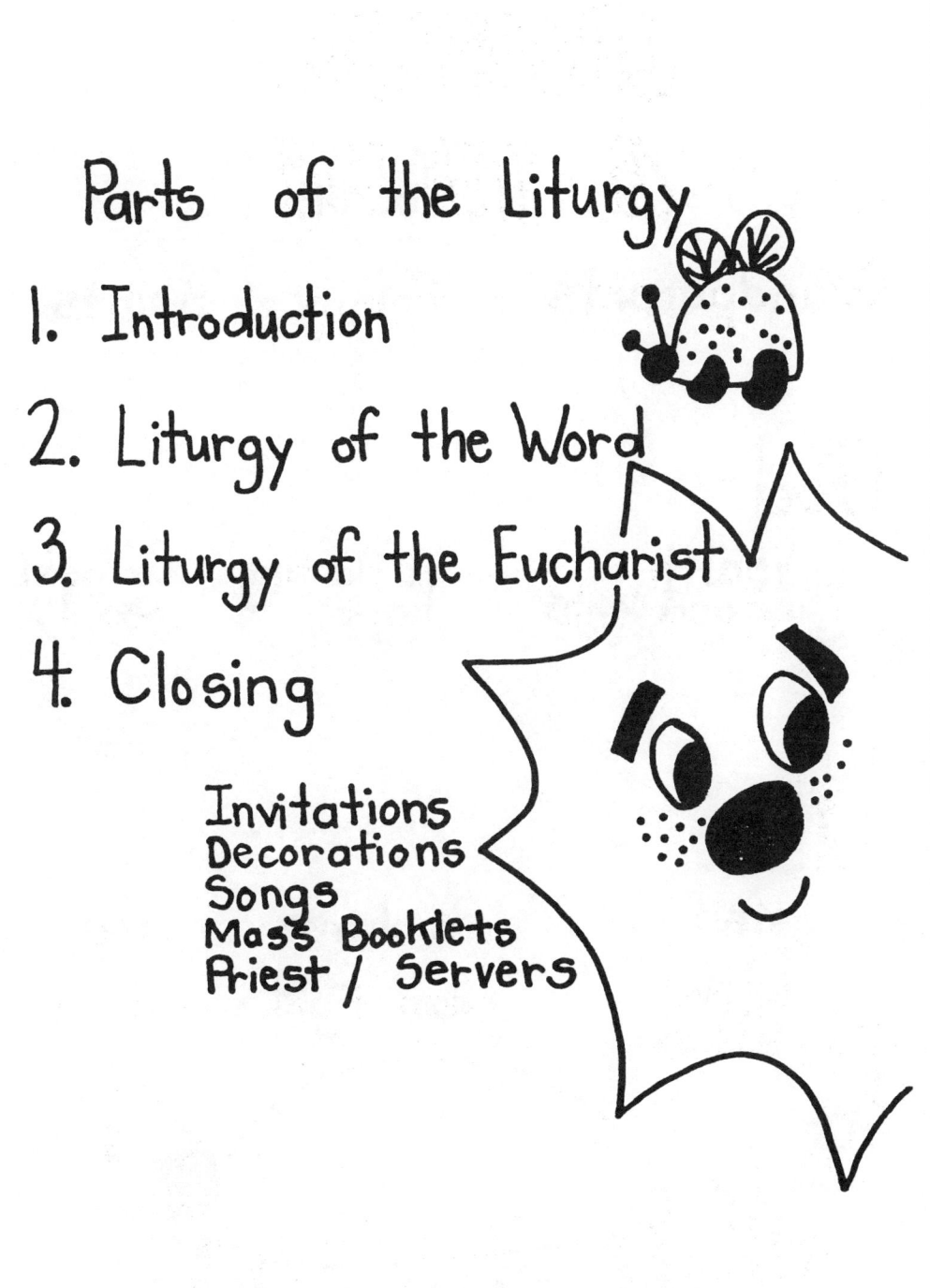

CHOOSING A THEME

Grandparents   family   Saints

God

health   no fighting   be good
no accidents   happy   people

Us

visit   do chores   study
write letters   don't fight   share

Theme Development Worksheet

Student Ideas...

_____

_____

_____

_____

Lead up Activities...

_____

_____

_____

Resources...

_____

_____

_____

Sample Invitation ... Primary

You are invited to the second grade liturgy on "Family"

Wednesday November 3 at 11 a.m.

Please come!

Love,
Grade Two

How to Plan Children's Liturgies

Parts of the Introduction

Songs
Greeting
Theme
Act of Penance
(Penitential Rite)
Lord Have Mercy
Gloria
Collect / Prayer

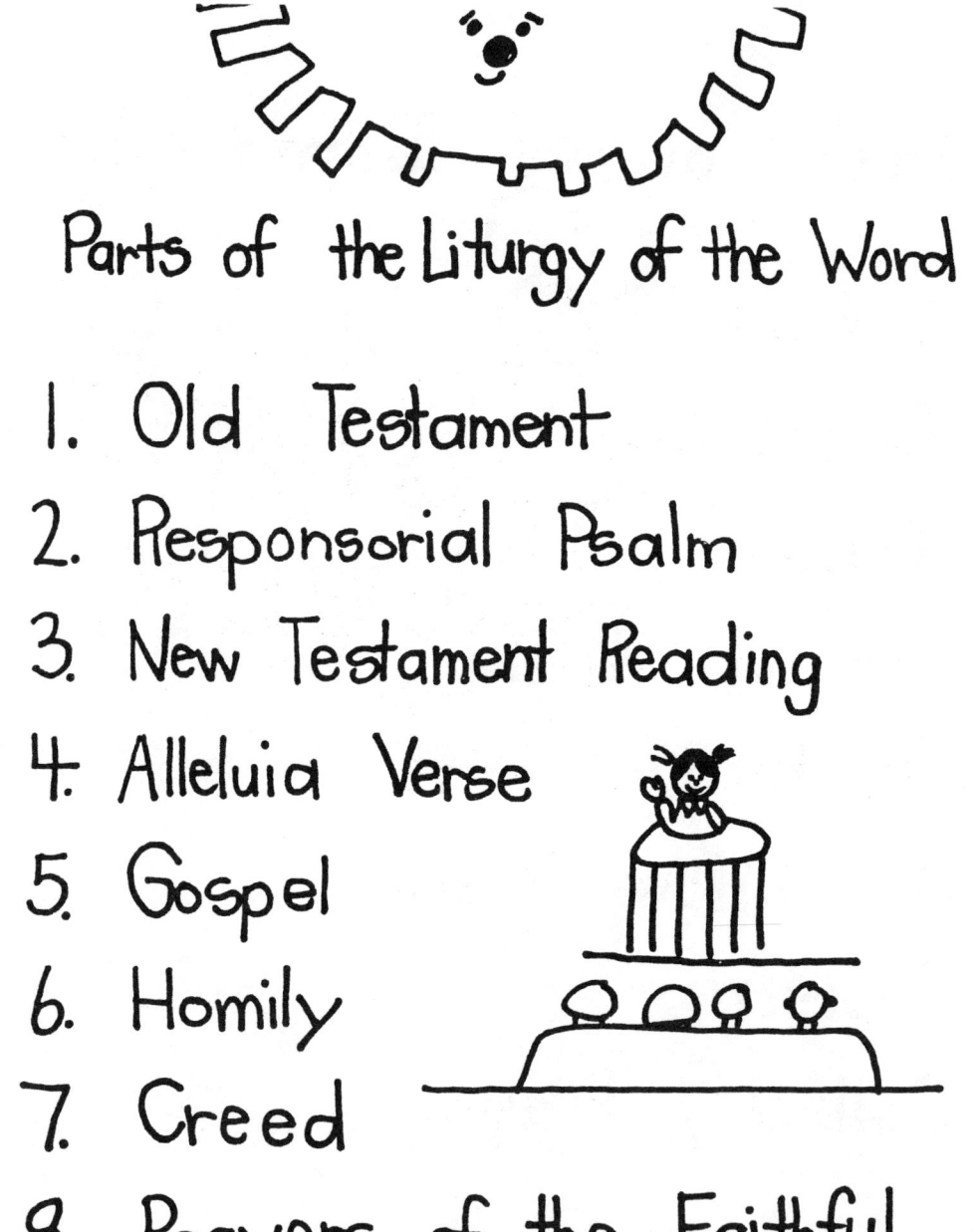

Parts of the Liturgy of the Word

1. Old Testament
2. Responsorial Psalm
3. New Testament Reading
4. Alleluia Verse
5. Gospel
6. Homily
7. Creed
8. Prayers of the Faithful

FIRST READING: The first reading is a story written by a second grader. She wanted us to know that our families can understand our feelings. She thinks the most important thing to remember is that our families love us no matter what!

How to Plan Children's Liturgies

Movie Making Notes...

Title: Story of Job — The Big Test

Words...	Scene...	Actresses & Actors
1. There was once a man... who feared God...	Job sitting with wife	Steve & Trena (Job & wife)
2. Did you notice Job? You spoil him! All he has is in your power	God sitting in garden — Satan dressed in black approaches	Sarah & Fred (God & Satan)
3.	cars whizzing by	
4. Your children are dead!	man knocks on door Job opens — sees newspaper "10 car pile-up"	Steve & Jose (Job & newsman)
5.		

PROCLAMATION OF THE WORD...THEME: FAMILY

FIRST READING: "My Family" (by William)

> I love my family very much. I fight with them. I get mad at them, but I don't mean to. If one of them were to die I don't know what I would do. Sometimes I get mad at my dad when he tells me to do something. When he tells me not to do something I get mad. I never really mean to get mad. We have a lot of fun too! We go to the park.
>
> Not too long ago my oldest sister went to live in Chicago. I did not want her to go. I don't know what I would do without my family. They mean a lot to me. That is why I love my family very much.

GOSPEL: Luke 9:46-48

> An argument started between them about which of them was the greatest. Jesus knew what thoughts were going through their minds, and he took a little child and set him by his side and then said to them, "Anyone who welcomes this little child in my name welcomes me; and anyone who welcomes me welcomes the one who sent me. For the least among you all, that is the one who is GREAT."

HOMILY:

> Based on a story written by Mary Kathryn Machado and Audrey Munoz about a boy named Tommy and his flower collection.

CREED:

Family is sisters, brothers, moms and dads.
We believe the people in our families care for each other.
We believe our families care about us.
We believe a family is some place to share our emotions.
We believe a family is getting along with others.
We believe family is counting on one another.
We believe family is trusting each other.
We believe in the family there is a lot of working.
We believe that a family is where happiness is brought on.
We believe family should be enjoyed and loved while its possible to do so.
We believe family is a place to come home to.
We believe what holds our family together is LOVE
          (Written by Junior High Students)

Family is mom, dad and their children.
We believe that we find love in our family.
We believe that grandpas, grandmas and other relatives make our family bigger and happier.
We believe families should help each other.
We believe families try to cheer you up when you are sad.
We believe that families take care of you when you are sick.
We believe that families try to keep us out of trouble.
We believe that our families want us.
We believe that you can be happy in a family.
We believe that our families try to hug us more than most people.

Another option for the Creed Ask a family to write a family creed.

PRESIDER: We introduce to you today the _____ family. They share with us their beliefs about our theme, "Family, a gift to the World."

MOTHER:

What I believe about my family is first, what they believe about me! The confidence and faith my own parents showed in me encouraged me to want to do my best and stick with my values and beliefs. A family is a support group — like an Indian tepee — all members are independently set in their spot but lean together and meet at a common point. Like the tepee, however, there is a necessary "breathing space" a hole through which smoke can escape for the LIFE of the family occurs inside the circle of supports not outside. My family for me immediately is my husband. What I believe in is his faith, his unwavering values, his conviction that our family is meant to be a firm building stone. I believe, I know, our family is rooted in Christ. The very fact that we have arrived "on this side" of the death of a 2 year old son, cancer in our oldest son and the suicide of a parent is a BLAZING message that our family is important as a FAMILY! It would be logical to be bitter, and inward but we are not. It is the Lord working in our tepee. I believe creating and maintaining a FAMILY is a full-time, life-long commitment.

SON:

> I believe my family is very special. I love my family and they love me. I think that we stand very well in our community. We have loving neighbors and good friends. God blesses my family very often with gifts of the Spirit. I love my family very much!

SON:

> I believe my family looks upon me as a boy who likes to try things. I like to do anything new (Within reason!). I believe my family loves each other. We may fight but we still love each other. My family foes to Mass every Sunday. So, I believe my family is very religious. My family is very, very, believable!

Parts of the Liturgy of the Eucharist

A. Preparation of the Gifts
   Procession
   Songs
   Prayers

B. Eucharistic Prayer
   Dialogue before Preface
   Preface
   Santus
   Eucharistic Prayer
   Proclamation of the Mystery of Faith
   Memorial Prayer

C. Communion Rite
   Our Father
   Rite of Peace
   Breaking of Bread
   Prayer Before Communion
   Holy Communion
   Post Communion Prayer

Parts of the Closing
Blessing
Dismissal

Traditional Responses

GREETING
PRESIDER: The grace of our Lord Jesus Christ and the love of God and the fellowship of the Holy Spirit be with you all.
ALL: **And also with you.**

PENITENTIAL RITE
ALL: **I confess to almighty God, and to you, my brothers and sisters, that I have sinned through my own fault in my thoughts and in my words, in what I have done, and in what I have failed to do; and I ask blessed Mary, ever virgin, all the angels and saints, and you, my brothers and sisters, to pray for me to the Lord our God.**
   or:
Lord have mercy. Christ have mercy. Lord have mercy.

GLORIA
ALL: **Glory to God in the highest, and peace to his people on earth. Lord, God, heavenly king, almighty God and Father, we worship you, we give you thanks, we praise you for your glory. Lord Jesus Christ, only son of the Father, receive our prayer. For you alone are the holy one, you alone are the Lord, you alone are the most high, Jesus Christ, with the Holy Spirit, in the glory of God the Father. Amen.**

OPENING PRAYER
ALL: **Amen.**

FIRST READING
PRESIDER: This is the word of the Lord.
ALL: **Thanks be to God.**

RESPONSORIAL PSALM (people's response varies)

SECOND READING
PRESIDER: This is the word of the Lord.
ALL: **Thanks be to God.**

GOSPEL
PRESIDER: Alleluia.
ALL: **Alleluia.**
PRESIDER: (Scripture verse)
ALL: **Alleluia.**
PRESIDER: The Lord be with you.
ALL: **And also with you.**
PRESIDER: A reading from the holy gospel according to _____ .
ALL: **Glory to you, Lord.**
PRESIDER: This is the gospel of the Lord.
ALL: **Praise to you, Lord Jesus Christ.**

PROFESSION OF FAITH
ALL: **I believe in God, the Father almighty, creator of heaven and earth: and in Jesus Christ, his only son our Lord, who was conceived by the Holy Spirit, born of the Virgin Mary, suffered under Pontius Pilate, was crucified, died, and was buried. He descended into Hell: the third day he arose again from the dead; he ascended into heaven, and sits at the right hand of God, the Father almighty: from thence he shall come to judge the living and the dead. We believe in the Holy Spirit, the holy catholic Church, the communion of saints, the forgiveness of sins, the resurrection of the body, and life everlasting. Amen.**

PRAYER OF THE FAITHFUL
PRESIDER: We pray to the Lord.
ALL: **Lord, hear our prayer.**
PRESIDER: (prayer varies)
ALL: **Amen.**

PREPARATION OF THE GIFTS

PRESIDER: Blessed are you, Lord, God of all creation. Through your goodness we have this bread to offer which earth had given and human hands have made. It will become for us the bread of life.

ALL: **Blessed be God forever.**

PRESIDER: Blessed are you, Lord, God of all creation. Through you goodness we have this wine to offer, fruit of the vine and work of human hands. It will become our spiritual drink.

ALL: **Blessed be God forever.**

PRAYER OVER THE GIFTS

PRESIDER: Pray, brethren that our sacrifice may be acceptable to God, the almighty Father.

ALL: **May the Lord accept the sacrifice at your hands for the praise and glory of his name, for our good and the good of all his church.**

PRESIDER: (prayer varies)

ALL: **Amen.**

EUCHARISTIC PRAYER

PRESIDER: The Lord be with you.

ALL: **And also with you.**

PRESIDER: Lift up your hearts.

ALL: **We lift them up to the Lord.**

PRESIDER: Let us give thanks to the Lord our God.

ALL: **It is right to give him thanks and praise.**

PRESIDER: (preface follows.)

ALL: **Holy, holy, holy Lord, God of power and might. Heaven and earth are full of your glory. Hosanna in the highest. Blest is he who comes in the name of the Lord. Hosanna in the highest.**

MYSTERY OF FAITH

ALL: **Christ has died, Christ is risen, Christ will come again.**

> *or:*
> **Dying you destroyed our death, rising you restored our life, Lord Jesus, come in glory.**
> *or:*
> **When we eat this bread and drink this cup, we proclaim your death, Lord Jesus, until you come in glory.**
> *or:*
> **Lord, by your cross and resurrection you have set us free. You are the Savior of the world.**

END OR EUCHARISTIC PRAYER

PRESIDER: Through him, with him, in him, in the unity of the Holy Spirit, all glory and honor is yours, almighty Father, for ever and ever.

ALL: **Amen.**

THE LORD'S PRAYER

ALL: **Our Father, who art in heaven, hallowed be thy name: thy kingdom come; thy will be done on earth as it is in heaven. Give us this day our daily bread; and forgive us our trespasses as we forgive those who trespass against us; and lead us not into temptation, but deliver us from evil.**

PRESIDER: Deliver us, Lord, from every evil, and grant us peace in our day. In your mercy keep us free from sin and protect us from all anxiety as we wait in joyful hope for the coming of our Savior, Jesus Christ.

ALL: **For the kingdom, the power and the glory are yours, now and for ever.**

SIGN OF PEACE

PRESIDER: Lord Jesus Christ, you said to your apostles: I leave you peace, my peace I give you. Look not on our sins, but on the faith of your Church, and grant us the peace and unity of your kingdom where you live for ever and ever.

ALL: **Amen.**
PRESIDER: The peace of the Lord be with you always.
ALL: **And also with you.**

BREAKING OF THE BREAD
ALL: **Lamb of God, you take away the sins of the world, have mercy on us. Lamb of God, you take away the sins of the world, have mercy on us. Lamb of God, you take away the sins of the world, Grant us peace.**

COMMUNION
PRESIDER: This is the Lamb of God who takes away the sins of the world. Happy are those who are called to his supper.
ALL: **Lord, I am not worthy to receive you, but only say the word and I shall be healed.**
PRESIDER: The body of Christ.
ALL: **Amen.**

PRAYER AFTER COMMUNION
PRESIDER: (prayer varies)
ALL: **Amen.**

BLESSING
PRESIDER: The Lord be with you.
ALL: **And also with you.**
PRESIDER: May almighty God bless you, the Father, and the Son, and the Holy Spirit.
ALL: **Amen.**

DISMISSAL
PRESIDER: The Mass is ended, go in peace.
ALL: **Thanks be to God.**

Additional Ideas

There are many creative ways to involve children in the celebration of the Mass. Finding the "right" prayer or song is not always possible. That is why I truly believe you have the greatest resource possible: the children themselves. If you can present them with the proper vehicle of expression, they will supply the right words and actions.

In my continuing experiences with children's liturgy, I find that children love to participate. And the more they participate, the better they become at fully integrating this prayer expression into their own lived experience. Involving youngsters at an early age provides them with a structure for future growth and development. Older children want to help. In the past two years, I have organized weekly prayer experiences for the entire school at St. William in Los Altos, and the older students have volunteered to assist and organize the younger students. They help the younger children to write their own prayers, to choose readings, and to practice songs. They have even made up their own "raps" to go along with special prayer intentions. When we are unable to have our weekly prayer experience, both boys and girls miss it.

Writing songs for the children's prayer is a good exercise for the older students. Suggest that they use tunes that most of the children know, such as "Down By the Station," "Frere Jacques," and "Reuben and Rachel." The *Wee Sing* series by Price / Stern and Sloan has music and many well-known tunes. Invite children to write words that fit their prayer experience. Rhyming dictionaries are available at most bookstores. Buy one to assist your group in completing their lyrics.

The *Joy of Signing* will help the children to make up their gestures for their songs. You do not need a gesture for every word. Find one gesture for the most meaningufl word in the line. Two gestures are usually plenty for any one line. More than that becomes too confusing. Gestures can also be used for words to the readings. The leader says a line and makes a gesture. The congregation repeats the line and gesture. Again, choose the most meaningful words to use gestures with. Do not try to sign every word.

Here are some sample songs, prayers, chants or "raps," and fingerplays. Many more are included in *Modern Liturgy* magazine.

Songs of Praise

Tune: "When Johnny Comes Marching Home Again"

> The Father of all who loved us first, we sing his praise.
> (Point to heaven / cross hands on heart / cup hands around mouth / raise hands)
> It is for Him we hunger and thirst; we sing his praise.
> (Point to heaven / touch mouth / cup hands around mouth / raise hands)
> We pray to Him and ask for Grace.
> (Fold hands in prayer / open palms and bow)
> He blesses us and shows his face.
> (Make the sign of the cross in the air / cup hands around face)
> We'll all sing praise to the Father who loved us first.
> (Cup hands around mouth / raise hands / cross hands on heart)

> It's Jesus who gave His life for us, We sing His praise (2x)
> (Touch palms with middle fingers / hold hands out, palms up / cup hands around mouth / raise hands)
> He lived as we on earth as man
> (Make a big circle with hands)
> We follow Him as best we can
> (Pull right hand with the left)
> We'll all sing praise to Jesus who died for us.
> (Cup hands around mouth / raise hands / touch palms with middle fingers / hold hands out, palms up)

> The Spirit was sent to share God's love, We sing His praise (2x)
> (Cross hands on hearts / cup hands around mouth / raise hands)
> He helps each one to better see
> (Point to others / cup hands around eyes)
> How we can live community
> (Cup hands, touch little fingers and rotate in a circle)
> We'll all sing praise to the Spirit who shares God's love
> (Cup hands around mouth / raise hands / cross hands over heart)

(Modern Liturgy, September '89)

Tune: "This Old Man"

1. Lift your voice, raise your heart
   Join our prayer and do your part

   Chorus: With a joyfilled song of praise
   Know that God will do
   All the things we ask Him to

2. With your friends, share your love
   Bring your needs to God above

3. Every day, do your best
   Help the poor and those oppressed

4. Raise your voice, Sing your praise
   Work for peace all of your days

(Modern Liturgy, September '89)

Penitential Rite

For the times we didn't listen...
(Make a circle on the left palm with the right index finger / safe sign / cup hands around ears)
...LORD HAVE MERCY.

(Strike breast with right fist)

For the times we were impatient with our friends and family...
(Make a circle on the left palm with the right index finger / safe sign / draw right thumb across lips to chin / hold hands out, palms up)
...CHRIST HAVE MERCY.

(Strike breast with right fist)

For the times we didn't accept responsibility for our actions...
(Make a circle on the left palm with the right index finger / safe sign / tap right shoulder with both hands / roll hands, right over left)
...LORD HAVE MERCY.

(Strike breast with right fist)

An echo pantomime: 1 Cor 13:4-13

A reading
(Palms up, little finger together)
from the first letter
(index finger up)
of Paul to the Corinthians
(Spread palms)
Love is patient
(Cross hands on heart)
Love is kind
(Roll hands over one another)
Love is not jealous
(Make baseball "safe" sign)
It does not put on airs
(Pick up and place object)
It is not snobbish
(Make baseball "safe" sign)
Love is never rude
(Touch lip and point to another)
It is not self-seeking
(Point to self with thumb / place hand over eyes)
It is not prone to anger
(Make baseball "safe" sign)
neither does it brood over injuries
(Point index fingers to head then together)
Love does not rejoice in what is wrong
(Pat chest with open hands)
but rejoices with the truth
(Place middle finger of right hand on left palm / move forward)
There is no limit to love's forbearance
(Hold palms facing each other)
to its trust,
(Pretend to hold on to a rope)
its hope,
(Clasp palms)
its power to endure
(Make two fists)
Love never fails
(Run right palm over left and off)
Prophecies will cease
(Touch little finger with index finger)

tongues will be silent
   (Put index finger over mouth)
knowledge will pass away
   (Move right hand away)
Our knowledge is imperfect
   (Pat forehead)
and our prophesing is imperfect
   (Point two fingers out)
When the perfect comes,
   (Make beckoning motion)
the imperfect will pass away
   (Move right hand away)
When I was a child,
   (Hold hands out at child's height)
I used to talk like a child,
   (Cup hands around mouth)
think like a child
   (Touch hands to head)
reason like a child
   (Make circle on forehead)
When I became a man
   (Hold hand out at man's height)
I put childish ways aside
   (Move hands away from body)
Now we see indistinctly,
   (Cup hands around eyes)
as in a mirror
   (Hold palms up in front of face)
then we shall see face to face
   (Place palms on chin)
my knowledge
   (Point to head)
is imperfect now
   (Place both bent hands before you at waist)
then I shall know even as I am known
   (Point to self with both hands)
There are in the end
   (Touch little finger with index finger)
three things that last
   (Hold up three fingers)

faith,
> (Touch forehead with index finger)

hope,
> (Clasp hands and loveplace hands on heart)

and the greatest
> (Throw both open hands up, palms facing forward)

of these is love
> (Cross palms on heart)

This is the word of the Lord
> (Hold palms up)

(Modern Liturgy, March '89)

Scripture Reading for Mary: Luke 1:26-38

NARRATOR: The angel Gabriel was sent from God to a town...named Nazareth, to a virgin betrothed to a man named Joseph, of the house of David. The virgin's name was Mary.

GABRIEL:
Rejoice O highly favored one
Soon you'll be blessed with a son!

NARRATOR: She was deeply troubled at his words, and wondered what his greeting meant.

GABRIEL:
Gentle Mary do not fear.
God loves and holds you very dear.
You shall conceive and bear a son
Name Him Jesus, holy one.
His dignity, it will be great.
The Son of God is his estate.

He will sit on David's throne.
For our sins he will atone.
Know His reign will never end.
This is the message that I send.

MARY: Tell me how this can be
As a man I never see?

GABRIEL:
The Holy Spirit He will come.
This work of God is just for some.
Hence your son will be well-known.
Elizabeth too has conceived a son
Even though most old have none.
So to God be most grateful.
For Him only is it possible.

MARY: I am here to serve the Lord
I say "yes" of my own accord.

NARRATOR: With that the angel left her.

(Modern Liturgy, May '89)

Thanksgiving Ideas

Tune: "Skip to My Lou"

> God the Father, Maker of light (3x)

(Hold right hand, thumb up, raise slowly. Touch fingertips to thumbs and open quickly)

> Thank you for all that's in our sight.

(Touch fingertips to lips and open palms. Cup hands around eyes.)

> Jesus Christ, God's only Son (3x)

(Touch middle fingers to opposite palms. Hold right hand, thumb up, raise slowly)

> Thank you for saving everyone

(Touch fingertips to lips and open palms. Cross fists, pull apart, turn wrists out)

> Holy Spirit, Gentle Dove (3x)

(Place right palm above left, move apart. Bring index fingers and thumbs of each hand together.)

> Thank You for sharing all your love.

(Touch fingertips to lips and open palms. Cross hands over heart)

(Modern Liturgy 15, no.8)

Tune: "Reuben and Rachel"

> Sing a song that shows thanksgiving
> For the gifts that you've received
> Bow your head and praise the God
> Who sends to you the things you need

(Modern Liturgy 13, no. 8)

Tune: "Down in the Valley"

> We join together, together we pray
> We praise the Father, Lord of each day
> Praise God and thank Him for sending His Son
> Jesus our Savior, Most Holy One
> Jesus our Savior, from up above,
> You sent the Spirit to fill us with love
> We join together, this is our prayer
> Bless us and keep us under your care.

Penitential Rite

LEADER: For the times we didn't say, "Thank you," Lord have mercy.

ALL SING: (Tune: "Frere Jacques")

> God our Father, God our Father
> Forgive us (2x)
> We believe in your love (2x)
> Grant us peace.

LEADER: For the times we tried and failed and wouldn't try again, Christ have mercy.

ALL SING: God our Father...

LEADER: For the times we didn't act as we should have, Lord have mercy.

ALL SING: God our Father...

Advent Ideas

A Fingerplay

> Four little children with one accord
> (Hold four fingers up)
> Sing and dance to praise the Lord
> (Cup hands around mouth, march in place, pointing index finger up.)
> The first one says, "The Lord is King!"
> (Hold up one finger, raise right arm)
> The second one says, "His praise we sing."
> (Hold up two fingers, cup hands around mouth.)
> The third one says, "God is the best."
> (Hold up three fingers, hold palms up.)
> The fourth one says, "His name is blest!"
> (Hold up four fingers, close fists and open them.)
> They teach us to love and how to care.
> (Touch heart, hold hands out to participants.)

(Modern Liturgy 15, no. 3)

Songs

Tune: "Rueben and Rachel"

> Jesus, Jesus, it is Advent
> Time to plan our lives anew
> Celebrate with Christmas greetings
> Work for peace in all we do
> Jesus, Jesus, it is Advent
> Time to share with others too
> All our dreams and hopes and visions
> Be good children just for You!

(Modern Liturgy 12, no. 8)

Tune: "O Come, O Come Emmanuel"

> For you, for You, oh God...we wait
> We light a candle marking the date
> Each week we'll pray that You come
> Into our lives, You are the Saving one
> Jesus, the Christ, the One we're waiting for
> Fill us with love, from You we ask no more

A Christmas Chant

> The story of Jesus we wish to tell
> It is a story we know so well
> The angels came to announce His birth
> Shepherds listened for all their worth
> No one believed that God would send
> A babe to reign until the end.
> But Mary believed the angel's word
> Joseph was scared at what he heard.
> The Son of God he must protect
> The angel said, "Now don't object."
> So Joseph took Mary to Bethlehem
> And Herod, the King, looked out for them.
> He wanted to kill the Holy One
> He told his troops, "It must be done."
> Three kings came from the far, far east
> To praise the God born with the least.
> A stable was the only throne
> This God would have for His first home.
> And gifts were brought to celebrate
> The savior's birth; it's not too late
> To bring your gift to God's own Son
> And sing your praise before we're done.
> The angels sang when He was born
> The shepards came on that first morn
> To honor and praise the King.
> So let us join with them and sing,
> Merry Christmas!

(Modern Liturgy 15, no. 9)

Lent Ideas

Song

Tune: "Skip to my Lou"

> Lent is here; let us pray to be good (3x)
>> (Place right index finger in left palm; fold hands in prayer)
>
> Acting as we know we should
>> (Turn completely around in a circle)
>
> We'll do our work and be kind to a friend (3x)
>> (Hit fists together; point to a friend)
>
> And let our love to all extend.
>> (Cross hands on heart; open palms out to all)
>
> Bless us, Father, and all that we think
>> (Make a cross in the air; touch head with hands)
>
> Bless us, Jesus, and all that we say.
>> (Make a cross in the air; cup hands around mouth)
>
> Bless us, Spirit, and all that we do
>> (Make a cross in the air; walk in place)
>
> Help us to grow up like You.
>> (Touch ankles and slowly raise hands to sky)

(Modern Liturgy 14, no. 3)

Blessing

LEADER: Please face a partner. Raise your hands, palms down and say, "May God, our Heavenly Father..."

ALL: May God our Heavenly Father...

LEADER: Lower arms to waist level and say, "Bless you with His peace every day."

ALL: Bless you with his peace every day

LEADER: Touch palms with middle fingers and say, "May Jesus, our redeemer..."

ALL: May Jesus, our redeemer...

LEADER: Place hands on heart and say, "Fill you with His love."

ALL: Fill you with his love.

LEADER: Stroke the backs of your hands and say, "May the Spirit, the Comforter..."

ALL: May the Spirit, the comforter...

LEADER: Hold the left hand with the right and pull forward, and say, "Guide you in the Christian life."

ALL: Guide you in the Christian life.

LEADER: Make the sign of the cross on your partner's forehead and say, "May Almighty God bless you, in the name of the Father, and of the Son, and of the Holy Spirit. Amen."

ALL: May almighty God bless you, in the name of the Father, and of the Son, and of the Holy Spirit. Amen.

(Modern Liturgy 13, no. 2)

Easter Ideas

Tune: "Down by the Station"

> On Holy Thursday / Jesus had a dinner
> He ate and drank with / all of his friends.
> He took some bread and he / blessed it and he broke it
> "This my body's / love God sends."

> Jesus took a cup of wine / and he blessed it.
> "This is my blood which was given / up for you"
> This was the night that / Judas betrayed Him
> Something true friends / wouldn't do.

> Good Friday Jesus / suffered and was beaten
> He offered up his life for / you and for me.
> Jesus is the Savior / One sent to redeem us
> He has died to / set us free.

> On Easter Sunday / early in the morning
> The friends of Jesus / went to his tomb
> There an angel said that / Jesus has risen
> This is just an / empty room.

(Modern Liturgy, March '89)

Scripture Reading with illustrations: Matthew 28:1-10

Divide participants into six groups. Decide to make a six-panel mural, six posters or pictures for photographing into slides. Ask each group to illustrate one of six scenes from Matthew 28:1-10:

1. Mary and Mary Magdalene at Jesus' tomb.
2. An angel appears to the two women in a flash of lightening.
3. The angel sits on the stone rolled back from the tomb with the guards on the ground.
4. The two women running to tell the Good News.
5. The women with Jesus.
6. The women embracing the feet of Jesus.

Post the mural or prepare the slides ahead of time.

Direct the participants' attention to the illustrations. If you made slides, show all six in succession. Then read the scripture and show each slide in sequence as it appears in the reading.

Finally, show the slides again as you reflect on the reading with the following prayers and times for spontaneous prayer...

(Show the first slide.)

LEADER:
Lord, please listen as we pray.
We come with Mary to the tomb to say...

> (Allow time for spontaneous sharing. What would you say to Jesus in Mary's place? If you were there with her?)

(Show the second slide.)

LEADER:
Lord, we see the angel appear in light.
Thank you for the times he's in our sight...

> (Again allow time for spontaneous sharing. When are you shaken? Stopped in your path? When are you aware of a power greater than your own?)

(Show the third slide.)

LEADER:
The angel speaks and tells us how
To find the Lord; we answer now.

> (Allow time for spontaneous sharing. Have you thought how different your life would be if Jesus had not been raised from the dead? When do you listen to the saving words of scripture?)

(Show the fourth slide.)

LEADER:
We're sent to tell all that we know
To rich and poor, both high and low.

>(Allow time for spontaneous sharing. Are you spreading the Good News of Jesus' redemption? How can you be a true disciple?)

(Show the fifth slide.)

LEADER:
And as we go, Jesus is there
To share our lives and every care.

>(Allow time for sharing. How do you know that Jesus is with you always? Do you recognize His presence in your life?)

(Show sixth slide.)

LEADER:
The women praise their God and bow.
By their example they teach us how.

>(Allow time for sharing. How do you praise God? What time do you give to praise God?)

ALL:
We praise you Lord each day we live
All praise and honor to You we give.

Planning an Entire School Celebration

To prepare a children's Mass which will include all the classes in your program, you might write a letter like this to each of the catechists:

Dear Colleague,

To prepare our all-school Mass celebration for the opening of school, I would appreciate your assistance. With your class, please write:

1. A prayer for the school community—write it on the back of this sheet.

Please ask each child to do a pencil drawing of God and their friends. Please do this on good paper as I will be using the drawings for the mass booklet.

2. An area we need to grow in (e.g., For the times we fought with friends)

For _____

3. What you "believe" you will learn about God this year.

We believe _____

4. A petition (e.g., For peace in our neighborhoods, we pray to the Lord.)

For _____

5. Choose a gift to bring to the altar that represents something the class will work on this year (e.g., friendship flower, star for fair play)

Gift: _____

Why it represents the class _____

6. Please write a blessing for your own class that you will read at Mass.

May God bless you, _____ graders, _____

_____

_____

Thank you for your help with this. I need it by _____.

When you receive the information from each of the catechists, you can collate it following the guide for the Mass on pages 14 and 15. Assign to each grade parts of the Mass such as Creed and Prayers of the Faithful. Let someone from each class read the class contribution. If you color code copies of the parts of the Mass, when it comes time for the Creed and Prayers of the Faithful and Offertory Procession you can invite the children with the appropriate cards to come forward at that time. If you have access to a computer, you can enlarge the children's parts for them. Give each participant a color-coded card with his/her reading. They can practice at home and bring the card to the celebration.

You will need to select songs for the Mass. Try to choose songs that most of the children know. Each of the catechists in your program will have to practice with their own group. If you choose to make up new words for well-known melodies, a short practice just prior to the celebration should suffice. Make sure the musician has the needed music.

Remember, the Mass is a celebration of our lives in Christ. A children's liturgy is a prayerful expression of the children. Everyone wants to do a good job when they read or have a special part to play. As a liturgist, you are the channel that helps make it happen. Be as comfortable as you can with the Mass and the children will follow your lead. Helping them to know the "proper" time to do their part will help them to find Jesus in the celebration of the Mass. Let us pray for one another...